3658

D0794113

Library
Oakland S.U.M.

The Minister's Marriage Handbook

By James L. Christensen

Funeral Services
The Minister's Service Handbook
The Complete Funeral Manual
Contemporary Worship Services
Funeral Services for Today
*The Minister's Church, Home, and
    Community Services Handbook*
Before Saying "I Do"
The Minister's Marriage Handbook
Difficult Funeral Services
The Complete Handbook for Ministers

The Minister's Marriage Handbook

James L. Christensen

Fleming H. Revell Company
Old Tappan, New Jersey

Scripture quotations identified RSV are from the Revised Standard Version of the Bible, copyrighted 1946, 1952, © 1971 and 1973.

Scripture quotations identified PHILLIPS are from THE NEW TESTAMENT IN MODERN ENGLISH, Revised Edition—J. B. Phillips, translator. © J. B. Phillips 1958, 1960, 1972. Used by permission of Macmillan Publishing Co., Inc.

Scripture quotations identified NEB are from the New English Bible. Copyright © The Delegates of the Oxford University Press and the Syndics of the Cambridge University Press, 1961, 1970. Reprinted by permission.

Quotations from THE BOOK OF COMMON PRAYER of the Episcopal Church in the United States, 1979.

Acknowledgment is made to the following for permission to reprint copyrighted material:

ABINGDON PRESS: Excerpts from "A SERVICE OF CHRISTIAN MARRIAGE." Copyright © 1979 by The United Methodist Publishing House. Used by permission; excerpts from A SERVICE OF CHRISTIAN MARRIAGE. Copyright © 1979 by Abingdon. Used by permission; excerpts from CELEBRATIONS FOR TODAY by Stephen Burgess and James D. Righter. Copyright © 1977 by Abingdon. Used by permission.

BOARD OF PUBLICATIONS OF THE CHRISTIAN REFORMED CHURCH: Excerpt copyright © 1981 from the SERVICE BOOK, PART TWO, BOARD OF PUBLICATIONS OF THE CHRISTIAN REFORMED CHURCH.

CHRISTIAN BOARD OF PUBLICATION: Excerpts from MANUAL OF FORMS FOR MINISTERS, by Benjamin L. Smith. Used by permission of CBP Press.

C.S.S. PUBLISHING COMPANY: Material from pages 172–180 and 211, 212 is taken from CONTEMPORARY WORSHIP SERVICES FOR SPECIAL DAYS, compiled by Ralph E. Dessem, Copyright © 1973 by C.S.S. Publishing Company, Lima, Ohio. Used with permission.

HARPER & ROW, PUBLISHERS INC.: Excerpt adapted from pp. 66–72 from THE SECRET OF A HAPPY MARRIAGE   By Roy A. Burkhart   Copyright © 1949 by Roy A. Burkhart; excerpt from pp. 33, 43, and 44 from EMILY POST'S COMPLETE BOOK OF WEDDING ETIQUETTE by Elizabeth Post   Copyright © 1982 by

Emily Post Institute; excerpt from pp. 94–101 from WOMEN AND WORSHIP: A Guide to Non-Sexist Hymns, Prayers, and Liturgies by Sharon Neufer Emswiler and Thomas Neufer Emswiler   Copyright © 1974 by Sharon Neufer Emswiler and Thomas Neufer Emswiler   Reprinted by permission of Harper & Row, Publishers, Inc.

JAMES R. HINE: Excerpts from *Grounds for Marriage*, by James R. Hine. Copyright, 1985, Interstate Printers and Publishers. Used by permission.

MACMILLAN PUB. CO. INC.: Excerpt reprinted with permission of Macmillan Publishing Company from LETTERS AND PAPERS FROM PRISON, Rev., Enlarged edn., by Dietrich Bonhoeffer. Copyright © 1953, 1967, 1971 by SCM Press Ltd.

MINISTERS COUNSELING SERVICE: Excerpt from lecture notes of James L. Cooper, Director, Ministers Counseling Service, Baptist General Convention of Texas.

NATIONAL COUNCIL OF THE CHURCHES OF CHRIST: Excerpt from PRE-MARITAL COUNSELING: A MANUAL OF SUGGESTIONS FOR MINISTERS used by permission of Program Committee for Professional Church Leadership, Division of Education & Ministry, National Council of Churches of Christ, USA, New York, NY 10115.

PULPIT DIGEST: Prayer by C. Neil Strait. From *Pulpit Digest*, June 1964. Copyright © 1964 by the Pulpit Digest Publishing Company. Used with permission from Pulpit Digest, Incorporated.

READER'S DIGEST: Excerpts from THE READER'S FAMILY LEGAL GUIDE, edited by Inge N. Dobelis, Copyright © 1981.

SCM PRESS LTD: Excerpt from CONTEMPORARY PRAYERS FOR PUBLIC WORSHIP ed., Caryl Micklem, used permission of SCM Press Ltd.

STANDARD PUBLISHING: Excerpt adapted from "A Forum of Solemnizing Marriage," from A Manual for Ministers, by R. C. Cave. © 1918. The Standard Publishing Company, Cincinnati, Ohio. Division of Standex International Corporation. Used by permission.

WESTMINISTER PRESS: Excerpt reprinted from *The Worshipbook—SERVICES*   Copyright © MCMLXX The Westminster Press. Reprinted and used by permission.

Library of Congress Cataloging in Publication Data

Christensen, James L.
  The minister's marriage handbook.

  Bibliography: p.
  1. Marriage—Religious aspects—Christianity—Handbooks,
manuals, etc. I. Title.
BV835.C467   1985   265'.5   85-2079
ISBN 0-8007-1424-5

Copyright © 1985 by James L. Christensen
Published by Fleming H. Revell Company,
Old Tappan, New Jersey
All rights reserved
Printed in the United States of America

Contents

Preface   11

of Common Prayer, A Community or Congregational Marriage Service, A Wedding Worship Service, A General Marriage Service

13 Contemporary Wedding Celebrations 169

A Marriage Celebration, Celebrating the Formation of the New Family, A Wedding Service in Modern English, A Contemporary Methodist Service for Christian Marriage, A Liberated Service

14 Special Wedding Circumstances 196

A Service for the Recognition of a Marriage or the Blessing of a Civil Marriage, Renewal of Wedding Vows, A Common-law Marriage, A Brief, Informal Marriage Service for a Second Marriage

15 Alternate Texts 204

Greetings, Opening Prayers, Homilies, Declaration of Intention, The Giving of Approval, Pastoral Wedding Prayers, Vows, Declaration of Marriage, Holy Communion, The Cup of Life and Love in Christ, Memory-Candle Lighting, Wedding Benedictions

TO
HEATHER AND CHRIS,

Our two adorable grandchildren, who fill our
hearts with joy, and for each we pray a happy,
enduring marriage

Preface

A wedding held in a church should be a Christian service of worship.

However, as George Hedley has written, "Nothing associated with the Church has been allowed to become so trivial, so irreligious, so much a display and so little a solemnization, as has the typical society wedding of our time. And the economically underprivileged, aping those who scarcely are their betters, have fallen into their own rather pathetic variations of the same bad taste and the same total lack of religious meaning."[1]

Persons planning weddings are inclined to consider what is pretty, glamorous, and impressive, rather than what is consistent and appropriate for a church marriage service. Too frequently others have been consulted for information about what is proper, when the church's minister should be the one to interpret the significance of marriage in a church.

Christian marriage is not *just* matrimony; it is *holy* matrimony. It is not an estate instituted by man; it is an estate instituted by God. Church is the proper place to celebrate Christian marriage; and the minister, as God's representative, is the key person in making more consistent and orderly the wedding service to the glory of God.

It is with the above conviction that this handbook has been prepared. At the outset, the author recognized the divergent viewpoints and practices of ministers, churches, and laymen. It is hoped, however, that the present material is sufficiently flexible, general, and nondogmatic as to be helpful, at least in part, to ministers of all persuasions.

JAMES L. CHRISTENSEN

11

The Minister's Marriage Handbook

Chapter One

How Marriage Has Changed

Since the rebellious years of the sixties, marriage has undergone major changes.

The institution of marriage was harshly criticized by a society concerned with the fulfillment of the self and resisting all traditional sex roles and authority patterns. The new slogans were "Do your own thing," and, "Be free from commitment." Marriage looked outmoded, because it seemed to negate independence. It was considered repressive.

A period of shocking upheaval and experimentation followed, which snowballed even into the present. Easy divorce, newly liberalized women, irresponsible men, and the Pill resulted in promiscuity of epidemic proportions, and many less than ideal marriages split asunder. Young people with expectations of instant and automatic gratification of all desires became disillusioned with marriage. They got out fast rather than giving and taking or adjusting and compromising to make their marriages work. It became fashionable to live together without marriage or to enter into open marriage. We were told by proponents of the new liberation that the old style of marriage was not only obsolete, but destructive to human integrity. It should go, they said.

That has not happened. While today many people remain single, and large numbers live together without marriage, the vast majority of people do marry from personal choice. There is a change in attitudes.

15

True, the revolution left its mark, for marriage has changed. The union of two people today is far different from the marriages of their parents and grandparents.

Today's people want more out of the marriage relationship. They seek a higher degree of emotional intimacy, as well as physical intimacy. They place great importance upon sharing innermost thoughts and feelings, which was difficult for the older, more reserved generations. The expectation in today's marriage is for each to foster the growth of the other in a mutually loving, supportive partnership. At the same time, they want a relationship that allows for individual freedom and that does not stifle either partner's separate goals and desires. This is the new ideal in marriage.

Such a relationship does not just happen. It is a difficult achievement. In the past, social mores and expectations governed a couple's marriage in most every aspect—sexual fidelity, daily routine, household decoration, proper attire. In marriage today the couple work out their own patterns regarding who works and who cooks, how finances are managed, where and how to live, sexual practices, relations with families, social and recreational participation. Every area must be discussed and agreed upon. Much negotiation and adjustment are inevitable with two individuals of different backgrounds, attitudes, and views. They are bound to conflict over some issues. Harmonious, long-enduring marriages call for conscious effort, mature spiritual graces, and effective skills. There is so much in our culture that dilutes the very ingredients of the social cement that holds marriages together. It is the purpose of this book to give some tools for the minister as he aids couples to prepare for this significant journey.

Chapter Two

Premarital Counseling

Most persons who marry believe their union will be blissful and divorce proof. Nearly 50 percent are disappointed. With premarital counseling, some such splits might have been averted, and some marriages might never have occurred.

Before marriage plans are set in concrete, a great deal of counseling needs to take place, preferably starting as soon as the couple is engaged. Four months before the wedding is an ideal time to begin such sessions. Led by the counselor-minister, the couple can begin to evaluate their relationship, understand what exclusive marriage really means, and be realistic about their expectations from marriage. To face potential difficulties constructively and make necessary adjustments before saying "I do" is most urgent for nearly every couple contemplating marriage. Happy and enduring relationships do not just happen. They are achieved as a result of mature and conscious effort.

The minister stands at the door to marriage, to explain the venture within, to warn the ill-prepared and obviously mismated, to tighten up the entrance exams; hopefully thereby he may help couples avert the troublesome storms and decrease the marriage dropout rate.

In going through a marriage ceremony and signing a license, two persons publicly assume the responsibility of a total commitment to each other. It bodes well for marriage that more couples are being married in a church than in the chambers of the justice of the peace, judge or mayor, because it indicates a greater emphasis today on the sacredness of marriage. Rather

17

than the sentimental, romantic aspects of marriage, the religious ceremonies and the wedding music increasingly direct thoughts to family, home, commitment, and God's love. The ceremony is conceived as a worship service before God, honoring Him, rather than primarily being an entertainment or a floral–gown display.

The minister must conceive of his duty as more than merely conducting a wedding service. He is more than a "marrying Sam" or the church's justice of the peace, who performs in a cold, uninterested manner, with his primary concern the size of the fee.

The minister's interest stretches far beyond the ceremony, to the couple's years of home and family life. Hence, his responsibility is to counsel the couple regarding all the factors involving happy marriage, so that a strong bond is cemented.

Of the many divorces occurring in our society, Nancy Piccione's research indicates 4.5 percent of them occur during the first year of marriage; 8.6 percent during the second year; 9.4 percent during the third year; 8.9 percent during the fourth year. The percentage continues to go down. After twenty-five years of marriage it reaches the all time low, with 1 percent.

The Reasons for Premarital Counseling

"An ounce of prevention is worth a pound of cure" underscores the necessity for premarital counseling. A few interviews before the wedding, conferring frankly and confidentially with the prospective bride and groom, may well prevent numerous difficulties and heartaches. One counselor stated: "I'd rather have thirty minutes with a couple before marriage than ten hours after the die is cast. It's more effective."

The late, longtime pastor of the First Congregational Church in Columbus, Ohio, Dr. Ray Burkhart, developed a remarkable premarital counseling program. He wrote: "It is my practice not to marry a couple without going through a process of study with them. The number of premarital interviews with a couple will depend largely on the degree of insight they show, their questions, and their interest. I ordinarily have three one-hour interviews with a couple before marriage and one subsequent to marriage. The first three are in my study. The fourth is in the couple's home after their marriage." He found the results to be so fruitful that he proposed: "A program of guidance . . . should be provided by every church, not only to meet its fullest ministry but also its choicest opportunity. . . ."

Premarital counseling provides the opportunity for establishing good relationships in a prospective marriage. Questions frequently focus on personality adjustments, personality differences, wedding plans, the honeymoon, physical adjustments, housing plans, religious differences, money and its management, emancipation from family, adjustments to new friendships, and in-laws.

Premarital counseling gives counselees the opportunity to ventilate fears, doubts, and wishes regarding marriage and each other, so that they recognize the importance of inner feelings in a marital relationship. It assists the couple to build and strengthen a realistic, positive philosophy toward marriage. By encouraging the couple to discuss their basic values, the minister aids them to realize that no marriage is perfect, and that all marriages require effort, compromise, unselfishness, and adjustment.

Premarital counseling should help determine the physical, intellectual, psychological, social, and spiritual compatibility of the couple and the potentials for happiness. If the situation indicates unusual or abnormal conditions, the minister may make referral to other specialists or agencies for assistance, or at least acquaint the couple with the professional resources available. He may discourage the couple from proceeding with marriage plans and thus eliminate the possible later tragedy of divorce.

Premarital-Counseling Resources

There can never be a stereotyped program of premarital counseling. Perhaps no two ministers use the same methods in detail. One may feel quite unprepared to undertake any extended program and will do little more than attempt a short talk with the couple. Another may offer a full course of guidance, including numerous hours of counseling and batteries of tests. Some refuse to marry couples who are not willing to complete the procedure they outline; the average minister, however, is not so exacting in his demands.

Scheduling two or three sessions with the couple is the most common practice. There are exceptions, where persons come to the minister wishing to be married at once. Unless the minister refuses to perform the ceremony, he can do little more than talk with them a few minutes, offering helpful advice, giving them booklets for further reading, and creating a climate of friendliness that will open the door for subsequent counseling. If a minister refuses to marry such people, in all probability they will seek out a justice of the peace, the minister thereby forfeiting the church's chance to counsel and guide them during their married life.

A variety of premarital counseling methods and devices may be used by the minister, including: interviews, written materials, psychological tests, films, group counseling, and referrals.

Interviews

The interview, the main method used by the marriage counselor, is a process by which the minister helps the couple talk about, feel about, and work through various areas of consideration, until they can objectively make their own decisions and plans.

Various schools of thought exist regarding the best method of interviewing. The "client-centered" (nondirective) and "counselor-centered" (directive) approaches are two that are common. In the *directive* method it is assumed that the couple confers with an expert, who listens to questions and answers them, or who listens to problems, interprets, and then offers possible solutions, making definite recommendations.

The *nondirective* approach is based on the philosophy that the counselees do the work and solve their own problems. The couple is asked questions, which they discuss in the presence of a sympathetic listener, the counselor. The purpose is to make them better understand themselves and their feelings and to more clearly chart their course.

Most ministers probably use the *eclectic* approach, a combination of the directive and nondirective approaches in interviewing. They feel that the personalities and demeanor of the counselees should determine the approach and that versatility is desirable.

The minister's role should be that of an experienced friend who is vitally interested in the welfare and happiness of the counselees. He seeks to enter into their thoughts, feelings, and plans. He does not assume a lecturing role, giving good advice; rather he seeks to stimulate them to express themselves and ask questions.

The marriage-counseling kit is a card-sorting device that serves as an icebreaker for couples who are being counseled and determines their opinions regarding marriage.

Written Materials

One of the most common tools of counseling used by the minister is written material. A young couple, with the wedding date set, may be concerned about the physical side of marriage. The minister may talk with them about their questions and concerns and then suggest two or three books that will give appropriate information.

Certain values are compromised, and also there are inherent hazards involved in the use of written materials in counseling. The counselor should be well acquainted with the literature he recommends so that he knows it is worthwhile and he is prepared for subsequent discussions that may arise from the reading. The books recommended should be individualized, taking into consideration the intellectual capacity, emotional stability, and readiness of the persons involved. People often take home printed literature, but fail to read it or ignore the unpleasant parts or that which is contrary to their beliefs. It is highly desirable for interviews to parallel the reading, so that the counselees have the opportunity to clarify their thinking and feelings regarding what is read.

A bibliography of appropriate literature is provided at the end of this text in the hope that it will be helpful in premarital counseling.

Psychological Tests

There are differences of opinion regarding the use of psychometric testing devices in marriage counseling. Although they have many limitations, they can be used to advantage.

There is an educational effect on the couple, realized from their considering many significant factors relating to their personalities and marriage. Problems may be located which might otherwise be overlooked. An overall view of marital potentials and needed adjustments are made more apparent. Among the tests recommended are: "Marriage Prediction Tests," by Burgess, Cottrell, and Terman; "Mate Selection Test," by Gilbert Appelhof; "Taylor-Johnson Temperament Analysis"; "Bernreuter Test"; "Minnesota Multiphasic Test"; "California Personality Test"; "Guilford-Zinn Temperament Survey"; and "Augustana Premarital Scoring Device." One of the most complete and most satisfactory testing instruments for personality inventory and marriage-happiness prediction is James R. Hine's manual, *Grounds for Marriage*. It is in easily usable form and is highly recommended for the minister's use. Although the statistical findings do not always apply to every individual case, yet as the counselor interprets and discusses the various responses to the tests they take on added meaning when impending marriage is considered. The minister must exercise caution, lest the tests lead to advice giving.

TAYLOR-JOHNSON TEMPERAMENT ANALYSIS PROFILE

The TJTA is a widely used diagnostic counseling instrument that serves as a convenient method of measuring a number of basic personality traits that influence interpersonal and person functioning and adjustments. (Published by Psychological Publications, Inc., 5300 Hollywood Blvd., Los Angeles, Calif. 90027.)

Nine traits are rated in contrast to their opposites, that is, nervous versus composed; depressive versus lighthearted, active-social versus quiet-withdrawn, expressive-responsive versus inhibited; sympathetic versus indifferent; subjective-self-absorbed versus objective-logical; dominant versus submissive; hostile versus tolerant; self-disciplined versus impulsive-uncontrolled.

This profile is especially appropriate for premarital counseling. It is based on years of statistical research and clinical experience. A manual guides in the administration of the test, yet it is strongly recommended, if not imperative, that a minister or counselor have at least six hours of specific professional training before using this test. Important decisions should not be made on the basis of this profile without confirmation of the results by other means.

Films

Several filmstrips and cassettes that have been carefully designed by experts in the family-counseling field are available. One of the most productive for ministers in premarital counseling is *The Good Marriage: It Doesn't Just Happen.* This program grows out of the conviction that marriage can be the most fulfilling of all human relationships if people are prepared to work for it. There are three color filmstrips and three tape cassettes or three twelve-inch long-playing records. (The material has been produced by Sunburst Department AW, 39 Washington Avenue, Pleasantville, N.Y., 10570, 1978, and is available in many public libraries.)

Part I, entitled "Marriage Is Getting Harder, But Better," illustrates how the expectations of marriage have changed dramatically over the years. A good marriage calls for hard work. Part II is called "The Person You Marry," and tells what the basic ingredients are for a stable marriage. Part III, "The First Year," introduces the couple to the concept of adjustment and working out differences from the start.

A leader's guide is included. Jean Robbins is the editor-in-chief.

A second worthy filmstrip program is entitled, *Newly Married Couples.* It has two cassettes, two filmstrips, a teacher's guide, and three attitude questionnaires. (This cassette-filmstrip program is a part of the Family Life series produced by Butterick Publishing Co., a division of the American Can Co., 708 Third Avenue, New York, N.Y. 10017, 1976. Betty Yonburg, chief consultant.)

Newly Married Couples examines marriage apart from romantic traditions. It gets right down to the "mundane business of daily living," examines the necessity for adjustment in marriage, and defines the areas in which problems requiring adjustment usually occur, such as sex, money, in-laws, mutual friends, religious differences, outside activities, and differing interests.

The three attitude questionnaires are: The Need for Adjustment, Patterns of Adjustment, and Quarreling.

Research assignments, role playing, and nonverbal role playing are techniques utilized in the sessions.

Group Counseling or Classes

Organizing small groups or classes under skilled leadership has proved to be an effective way of helping prospective husbands and wives prepare for marriage. Group counseling provides an opportunity to work through fears and hostilities, releasing any conflicts in feelings. Release is accomplished through discussion, ventilation of feelings, as well as through "passive" participation (feeling deeply as the conflicts of others are heard). The necessary insight and support to reshape attitudes, modify behavior, deal with problems in new ways, and accomplish the necessary personality growth for more satisfactory marriage adjustment may result from this process.

The minister may be able, also, in his Sunday sermons to help persons preparing for marriage.

Referrals

One effective function of the minister-counselor is giving a referral to another qualified person and helping the counselee understand and accept the referral.

Among those to whom referrals may be made are: physician, lawyer, professional marriage counselor, and psychiatrist or marriage-counseling center.

During the initial interview the minister should suggest that the persons planning marriage have an interview with a physician. The minister can make the couple aware of the possible benefits of the physician's interview and delineate the areas about which they should inquire, such as: complete medical examination of both partners, including gynecological and urological, and a careful, nontraumatizing pelvic examination of the girl; blood analyses, including blood count, RH typing, and blood serology; discussion of factors contributing to adequate and satisfactory sexual adjustment; birth-control information, if desired; discussion of hereditary concerns;

discussion of anatomy and physiology of the reproductive system; sound information to dispel distorted ideas and reduce fears regarding childbirth; and proper referral if special attention is needed by a specialist.

Usually, young couples marrying for the first time have no reason to seek legal counsel. However, there are cases of handling private income, legacies, wills, and property which might require legal assistance. In the event of unusual circumstances regarding the legality of a marriage due to foreign citizenship, race, or relationship, the minister would be wise to make a referral to a lawyer.

In cases of remarriage, there may be legal problems concerning the previous marriage, spouse, or children. Older persons remarrying or even marrying for the first time frequently have property, possessions, businesses, or other assets that they want to transfer, divide, or will in a specific manner. The lawyer is in a position to assist in premarital counseling and thus prevent unhappiness and serious family complications in years ahead.

Many cities of America are blessed with marriage-counseling centers. Although their main function is to assist couples who are already married and have marital difficulties, they also provide premarital assistance. Usually there are several persons who represent different special services who are available for counsel.

If the minister recognizes abnormal emotional problems related to courtship and marriage, personality conflicts, or symptoms of neurosis or psychosis, a direct referral to a psychiatrist for evaluation or consultation is expedient. In some cases, the psychiatrist and minister may collaborate, with joint interviews and consultation, for the reorganization of the inner lives of the prospective mates.

Areas to Be Covered

There are many areas of information that need to be covered for a successful premarital-counseling program. No fixed outline can be predetermined for every couple, however, for the minister's degree of knowledge of each will vary, plus the fact that the needs of each person will vary. It is not possible for the pastor to plan exactly what will be said in the counseling session; he must be ready for anything. Nevertheless, by proper lead questions, the minister can direct conversations to the basic issues that most couples should confront before marriage. Among the areas that should be discussed are:

> The place of the family in our changing cultures
> Understanding of masculine and feminine roles
> Relationship of vocational choice to adjustment in family life
> The problems of two careers
> Meaning and value of money and principles of family finance
> Understanding sex and its place in Christian marriage
> Parenthood
> Relationship to in-laws
> Relationship to church and home
> Capacity and methods of resolving problems
> Ways of continued growth personally and in relationship

Degree of Acquaintance and Compatibility

Research studies have shown that marriages preceded by long acquaintance have a much better chance of success than those of persons who marry hastily. Without thorough acquaintance, it can be little more than a guess whether there is a reasonable assurance of compatibility of temperament and personality. Persons who have known each other for a long time have probably already made many of the major adjustments of personality necessary.

Premarital counseling should determine whether the prospective partners have the similar tastes, wishes, habits, and ideals sufficient to provide a broad basis of understanding and enduring companionship; whether they enjoy the same pursuits, have the same interests, and are able to appreciate the same friends; whether they know how to disagree without unkindness, control their anger, and find true harmony of spirit and respect in spite of differences. A broad base of mutuality can be developed, providing the two people want the same things from life and are willing to go in the same direction. The main problems of adjustment should become apparent in the counseling process.

The Maturity of Love

While love is the greatest thing in marriage, it is far deeper and more inclusive than many seeking marriage realize. If love is interpreted only as a sentimental feeling, then it will die when the romantic glamour fades. If it is only physical attraction, then it will fade when the body loses its beauty.

What does love involve for each marriage partner? What is the concept of love? Have the persons gone beyond mere infatuation? Have they achieved a creative partnership?

Answers to these questions the minister should seek to have expressed; he should emphasize that marriage is a process of growth together, and that love grows deeper and more profound as the years pass. In mature love, one has the habit of thinking of the other more than of "self."

Religious Backgrounds

Among the most important explorations in premarital interviewing are the religious backgrounds and intentions of the two persons. Couples who are bound together in God and in common religious experiences have a stability that is not known to those whose marriages are based merely on secular attitudes. The prospect for a happy and enduring marriage is three times greater when both persons are actively associated with the church. The emotions that urge people into marriage are in danger of withering unless they have strong roots in the entire nature of the individual—physical, mental, and spiritual.

The minister should make sure that persons from diverse religious backgrounds understand the differences involved and the potential difficulties that may arise; this is especially true when the persons involved are of Roman Catholic and Protestant, Christian and Jewish, and Christian and secular backgrounds. He should lead them to see how religion will bless and help their marriage, as well as how their home can be a cell in God's Kingdom on earth. The minister should help the couple work toward a common church affiliation before marriage, if at all possible. They may wish to attend the church of the person who is most active, or they may find it difficult to decide between churches, since both are equally committed. Theirs will be a new family, distinct and unique. The agreement on church affiliation needs to be made, based not only on the religious patterns of the homes from which they have come, but also on consideration of the welfare of the new home. It should be a mutually agreeable solution, which may require a spirit of compromise by both persons in order to find a mutually acceptable church. The important factor is that they recognize in religious faith and practice a means of deeper communion with each other.

The minister should help them to recognize that God is the author and sustainer of the love that binds man and wife together.

Sex Adjustment

Some ministers believe that the subject of sex should receive the major attention in premarital counseling. It is true that sex is a basic and important element in marriage. Satisfactory physical adjustments and wholesome attitudes toward sex are essential for mental, social, and spiritual adjustments. Some attention does need to be given this subject in counseling in order that fears may be allayed or correct and proper information given. The sex relationship in Christian marriage is not the mere expression of physical passion and biological necessity. It is the symbol of the complete dedication of a man and woman to each other. An expression of self-giving and trust, sex is the part of one's value system that demonstrates the inner essence of marriage. It is appropriate for the minister to deal with the sex relationship as part of spiritual unity and self-giving in marriage. Much ignorance, erroneous information, prudishness, and gratification seeking contribute to maladjustment. Although this subject need not be the main, or only, subject of premarital counseling, it must not be treated artificially or neglected, with the assumption that any adjustment will be made automatically.

Some ministers feel that the treatment of this question can

be done best through printed material, carefully chosen and perhaps given by the minister, with a brief explanation. Still other ministers feel that the sexual aspect of marriage can be better and more normally handled by a well-chosen physician, who can determine the physical elements of fitness and can assist in giving birth-control advice.

Finances

One of the most difficult adjustments for the newly married may be financial. A large number of marital problems (that I have confronted in my ministry, at least) have some relationship to money. Usually, each unmarried person has the habit of making his or her own decisions regarding the spending of money, perhaps with no conscious budget limitations. In marriage, however, there must be teamwork and an unselfish consideration of each other. The financial problem is not always that there is an insufficient amount of money to spend; it is more often a question of common purpose, of wise spending, of curbing selfishness, and of using money in such a way that each will feel that the other is considerate.

The minister can encourage a plan for setting up a budget in order to avoid financial misunderstandings and difficulties. The couple has to achieve agreement about what they want, how to plan for it, and how to spend.

Decisions should be made regarding whether the wife should work, what sort of insurance program they should start, whether they should purchase on credit, whether there is sufficient income to get started, who should pay the bills, and what kind of bank account to open.

I counsel husbands and wives to have separate, individual bank accounts. To provide access to each other's accounts in case of emergency, each can give the other either a limited or a full power of attorney. Some persons say: "My wife and I trust each other, so we have a joint bank account. It is a symbol of our unity." Fine. However, the joint account, technically, has inherent difficulties that may not be recognized. In the case of the death of one party to the account, the other party may be barred from any access to it until it has been released by the state in which the bank is located. The state's tax agents want to make sure they collect full inheritance taxes on such accounts, and far from assuming that the account belongs to the survivor, they are likely to take the position that it belonged entirely to the decedent and is therefore fully subject to tax. Not all the defects of a joint account are postmortem. Each party to the account must keep the other aware of all deposits and all checks drawn, or it is not possible to keep track of the balance on hand.

Examples of Premarital Counseling Procedures

Procedures for premarital counseling are as varied as the number of ministers. Each has a different manner, and usually develops his own techniques, adapting them to the needs of the particular couple he is interviewing. It is desirable to have several unhurried periods to evaluate a particular method, and to know the procedures of other ministers who excel in this area.

Dr. James Cooper[1]

INTERVIEW ONE

1. Establish rapport, friendly atmosphere.
2. Fill in form by asking general family and background information, number of brothers and sisters; how they get along with their father, assessment of parent's marriage happiness, how long they have known each other, how long engaged.
3. Ask each one to enumerate:
   What attracted you to the other?
   What do you really like about the other?
4. Then ask bride-to-be, "What things does he do that 'bugs' you?"
5. Then ask groom, "What things does she do that irritate you?" Discuss these awhile.

ASSIGNMENT FOR NEXT SESSION

1. Read and interpret the following Scriptures: Matthew 19:3–9; 1 Corinthians 13; Ephesians 5:21–6:4. Be prepared to discuss them at second interview.

INTERVIEW TWO

1. Discuss questions left over or that have arisen from Session One.
2. Discuss the Scripture assignments and the meaning of each.
3. Explore role expectations (a) How do you conceive of your role as a wife? Where did you get this concept of a wife? (b) How do you conceive of your role as a husband? Where did you get this concept of a husband?
   (c) To groom: Does her concept of the wife's role differ in any way with your concept? (d) To bride: Does his concept of the husband's role differ in any way with your concept?

ASSIGNMENT FOR NEXT SESSION

1. Continue to dialogue with each other about your expectations.
2. Each one make an independent list from your own observations of other marriages on, "What are some of the problem areas of marital adjustment?"

INTERVIEW THREE

1. Discuss leftover questions from Session Two.
2. Compare the lists of marriage problem areas.
3. What other areas did you overlook?
4. What adjustments can be made before marriage in these areas?

ASSIGNMENT FOR NEXT SESSION

1. List all available resources and tools for marital adjustment and harmony.
2. Prepare your family budget.

INTERVIEW FOUR

1. Discuss the report of tools for marital adjustment and harmony.

2. Look over and discuss the proposed budget.
3. Discuss any leftover questions.
4. Talk about the type of wedding, the details in planning, and the content of ceremony.
5. Have a prayer of blessing.

INTERVIEW FIVE

1. Held two weeks after marriage.
2. Discuss anything that may surface.

Oliver M. Butterfield

Dr. Oliver M. Butterfield gives a list of questions to the persons to be married. From this, he asks them to select those which they would like to talk about. His list is as follows:

1. How long acquainted? Where did you meet? How well acquainted?
2. How do your families feel about the match?
3. Where do you expect to live after marriage?
4. What are your business connections? Ambitions? Permanence? Will the wife work after marriage? How long?
5. Have you agreed on a practical budget? Who will keep the books?
6. Does either of you carry life insurance?
7. Has either of you health problems to face? How long since you had physical examinations? Do you plan to have examinations before marriage?
8. Social life and recreation—Do you have the same set of friends in general? Does either of you dislike some of the other's friends? What amusements or hobbies do you have in common? Separately? How do you get on with each other's relatives?
9. Home life and plans—How do you agree on likes and dislikes in food? Music? Clothes (color schemes, etc.)? Have you ambitions to own your own home?
10. Sex information and reading—What have you read on the sexual aspects of marriage? Would you like the name of a reliable physician whom you could consult

if you wished to do so? Are you agreed about children? Do you have reliable information on birth control?

11. Miscellaneous inquiries—Anxieties about problems of differences in temperament, heredity, age, education, religion, family dominance, travel.

12. Religious life and attitudes—What were the religious habits and attitudes of your parents? Do you personally differ from your parents in such matters? What are your plans for religious life after marriage?

13. Dismissal, with some plan for subsequent contacts.[2]

James L. Christensen

Marriage preparation classes are scheduled once or twice each year, to which couples contemplating marriage are invited. Both prospective brides and grooms are invited to attend. The text used for the six session course is my book *Before Saying "I Do."*

Couples who have not attended the class and who wish to be married by me are asked to attend four personal interviews, beginning four or five months before the expected wedding time. If the latter attended a class series, then only one interview is required. The first three interviews are one or two weeks apart and ideally accomplished before the detailed wedding plans are made.

Interview one is consumed in filling out the "Marriage Information Record" (*see* page 35). Then discuss in an informal way:

How long have you known the person you intend to marry?

How did you meet? What attracted you to the other?

Has either of you been married before?

What factors lead you to believe you can have a happy married life together?

How would you classify your parents' attitude toward your intentions?

If there is an objection to the marriage, what are the grounds?

How would you classify the married life of your parents?

Each is drawn into the discussion by directed questions.

Each is then presented with my book *Before Saying "I Do"* as a gift from the church. I ask them to turn with me in the book to Reflection Guide 1, Do You Really Want to Marry?; Guide 2, The Case for Exclusive Marriage; Guide 3, Marrying Again (for those who have been previously married); Guide 4, Before Becoming Too Emotionally Involved; Guide 5, The Spiritual Dimensions in Marriage. The chapters following each guide are assigned reading for the next session.

INTERVIEW TWO

This session is consumed primarily in discussing the first six chapters and the questions in Reflection Guides 1, 2, 4, and 5. By this session each should be sufficiently relaxed that they will talk freely and honestly. Following the discussion, they are asked to turn to Reflection Guides 6–10. Again they are assigned the reading of the chapters following each guide and to come to the next session prepared to discuss their feelings. A brief film, *Marriage Is Getting Harder, but Better* is shown and discussed after the assignment.

INTERVIEW THREE

This session begins with an open and frank discussion of the previously assigned material. At this time the Premarital Scoring Inventory is taken, tabulated, and discussed. Potential problem areas may be diplomatically noted, and I suggest that they work in this area and begin making whatever adjustments are possible. The crucial question is, "Are each of you willing to continue plans for marriage and to give 100 percent to make it succeed?"

A second film, *The Person You Marry,* is shown and discussed.

INTERVIEW FOUR

The final session before marriage (twelve weeks in advance) will deal with chapter 15, "Marriage Laws," chapter 12, "The Marriage Ceremony," which deals with its content and interpretation (a copy is given to the couple); and chapter 11, "Planning the Wedding." Each may be read together.

A copy of a twelve-week preparation schedule is given to each. Then the Details-of-Wedding Form is filled out—one for the couple and one for the bride. Other information—a reading list, responsibilities of participants, church's policy, and costs are given. An appointment is made for the bride and her mother to meet with me. The final wedding date, time, and place are scheduled. Chapters 13 and 14 are assigned for reading before the wedding. Film 3, *The First Year,* is shown. A prayer is given, which concludes the premarital counseling sessions with the couples.

Hopefully the meeting with the bride and her mother will be following the four sessions. If time is shorter, the meeting with the mother may need to be much earlier, as well as an adjustment of the content of session four into an earlier session.

During the session with the mother the following details are confirmed:

1. The date, time, and place for the wedding, rehearsal, wedding dinner, and reception are made.
2. Fees and the church's policies are discussed.
3. The church building is reserved, with a deposit made.
4. The dates and times are confirmed with all the staff participants (including the minister, organist, caterers, singers, custodian) by the church secretary and are entered into their appointment books.
5. Various financial responsibilities of the bride's family and the groom's family are discussed.
6. Floral decorations, wedding pictures, wedding music, communion, special requests, special problems, and rehearsal procedures are discussed.

Clergyman's Marriage Information and Permanent Record[3]

Wedding of: Date of Application _____
_____   Time of Wedding _____
_____   Church or Chapel _____
File No. _____   Officiating Clergyman _____
Preliminary question: "Has either of you been married before?" _____ (Note: In case of applicant's previous marriage, special arrangements must be made, due to Church laws.)

QUESTIONS TO ASK THE BRIDE
1. Full name of bride _____
2. Present address _____ Phone no. _____
3. Residence after marriage _____
4. At what permanent address may you always be reached?
   _____
5. Occupation _____ Age _____
6. Place of birth _____
7. Father's name _____ Mother's maiden name _____
8. How would you classify the married life of your parents?
   Extremely happy _____ Moderately happy _____
   Satisfactory _____ Unsatisfactory _____
                    Divorced _____
9. Church membership _____ Attend where? _____
   Active? _____
10. How long have you known the person you intend to
    marry? _____
11. How would you classify your parents' attitude toward your
    coming marriage?
    Enthusiastic: Father _____ Mother _____
    Favorable: Father _____ Mother _____
    Mild approval: Father _____ Mother _____
    Consent with reservations: Father _____ Mother _____
    Object to marriage: Father _____ Mother _____
12. If there is an objection to the marriage, what are the
    grounds? _____
13. What factors lead you to believe you will have a happy
    married life together? _____
14. What preparation have you made for marriage by way of
    study courses, reading, or consultations with doctor, min-
    ister, or other counselor? _____
    _____
15. When you see your doctor, will you have a thorough phys-
    ical examination in preparation for marriage? _____
    A talk with him? _____

QUESTIONS TO ASK THE GROOM
1. Full name of groom _____
2. Present address _____ Phone no. _____
3. At what permanent address may you always be reached?
   _____

4. Occupation _____ Age _____
5. Place of birth _____
6. Father's name _____ Mother's maiden name_____
7. How would you classify the married life of your parents?
Extremely happy _____ Moderately happy _____
Satisfactory _____ Unsatisfactory _____
Divorced _____
8. Church membership _____ Attend where? _____
9. How would you classify your parents' attitude toward your marriage?
Enthusiastic: Father _____ Mother _____
Favorable: Father _____ Mother _____
Mild approval: Father _____ Mother _____
Consent with reservations: Father _____ Mother _____
Object to marriage: Father _____ Mother _____
10. If there is an objection to the marriage, what are the grounds? _____

_____
11. What factors lead you to believe that you will have a happy married life together? _____
12. What preparation have you made for marriage by way of study courses, reading, or consultations with doctor, minister, or other counselor? _____

_____
13. When you see a doctor, will you have a thorough physical examination in preparation for marriage? _____
A talk with him? _____

QUESTIONS TO ASK THE COUPLE
Are you willing to enter into a counseling program, which involves private study and at least two more interviews with the counselor? _____ Dates for further conferences _____

Dissuading Marriage

In some cases, the minister will feel it necessary to dissuade people from marrying. Especially is this true when: the couple is very young; the plan to marry seems hasty and ill-considered; the persons are openly profane or drunk; there is serious emotional instability, a high incidence of mental disease in the families, or active tuberculosis or venereal disease; or medical examinations reveal that for some reason normal sex relations will not be possible. The minister cannot sidestep these factors or just hope that no difficulties will arise. He has a responsibility to the persons themselves, to society, and to his own conscience.

Dissuading marriage is a difficult matter. It is doubtful that the minister ought to conclude dogmatically and arbitrarily that the marriage cannot succeed (the couple might prove him wrong); however, he can express his concerns and urge that they delay plans for marriage for further counsel and research, which might bring them to the conclusion that the union would be unwise. The minister might say: "In view of this unsolved problem, do you not think it would be better for all concerned to delay your marriage until you have been able to think these matters through?" The minister does a tragic disservice by marrying the obviously mismated, and he does any couple a service by getting them to postpone an ill-considered step.

The minister should not play God, however. The final decision rests with the couple. The responsibility becomes theirs.

The Divorced Person Seeking Remarriage

Should a minister conduct the ceremony for a divorced person? This is becoming an increasingly prevalent problem because of the great number of divorces.

In some denominations, the minister is refrained explicitly from remarrying those who are divorced by a specific law in his church. Some pastors have the personal policy of refusing to marry all divorced persons, it being a matter of conscience—to marry them, they feel, would make them a party to violation of New Testament teaching.

However, others feel that this simple solution may involve a cruel injustice and is too arbitrary. It would seem to some that each case should be considered on its merits.

Admittedly, the Christian ideal is marriage for life; yet we live in an unideal world. Many mistakes and immature marriage decisions are made. Divorce, though sinful, is often the lesser of two evils. It is sinful, yet not unpardonable, wherein there is a humble, contrite spirit of remorse, and a genuine repentance.

The minister is concerned both to help the persons who come to him and to maintain Christian standards. Where there has been a first failure, the minister should certainly not pass over the matter with the mere hope that the new venture will be more successful. Rather, by counseling, he should help the person who has made one domestic failure to understand the destructive factors that wrecked the first marriage and to avoid them in the second. A divorced person should develop insight into the causes of the first failure and determine to avoid such mistakes in the future, before even considering remarriage. When such a spirit is manifested by one seeking remarriage, and if sufficient time has elapsed for maturing and emotional freedom to develop, it might be very unwise for the church to close the door on a remarriage. It might be most spiritually damaging to one seeking recovery and an honorable life. Some ministers, therefore, without condoning divorce or considering it lightly, attempt to determine the factors that caused the divorce and whether the attitudes and habits which contributed to the first breakdown have been overcome, so as not to undo a second marriage. The minister should try to determine the sincerity, the maturity, and the depth of repentance of the party seeking remarriage before turning him or her away. In the spirit of prayer for God's guidance and His forgiveness, the decision can be made.

Chapter Three

Marriage Laws

There is a notable and regrettable lack of uniformity from state to state in marriage laws. For the minister who serves in several states, it is difficult, nevertheless important, to keep up with the amazing variety of statutes regulating marriage.

There are variations regarding persons who are permitted to marry, the information required on the application license, the period of advance notice, and almost every facet of procedure and requirement.

Since the minister is sought out for early counsel, and stands as a "guard" at the "marriage doors," here is some of the pertinent information regarding general marriage laws.

Who May Legally Officiate at a Wedding?

Nearly all states permit either civil or religious authorities to solemnize marriages. Only one state, Maryland, restricts the right to religious officiants only.

Among the civil officers authorized to solemnize marriage, the justices of the peace are the ones who most commonly perform marriages, although governors, mayors, judges, and, in some places, notary publics, may officiate.

About three-fourths of all marriages in the United States are performed by religious officiants, because most people consider marriage a sacred undertaking. Also, the civil ceremony frequently is devoid of reverence, beauty, and dignity.

Upon moving to a new state, it is well for the minister to visit the county clerk, to familiarize himself with all the laws in question. If it is necessary to register, he should do so immediately, declaring his credentials. It is required that a clergyman be registered either in the county clerk's office where he serves or in some county of the state.

Any lawyer could assist in answering legal questions that occur.

Is a Blood Test Required?

In most states, a Wasserman or other standard laboratory blood test is required of persons planning to marry, showing freedom from venereal disease. The test can be given by a licensed physician within forty days before marriage, with the laboratory work done by the state department of health or a laboratory approved by it.

A medical certificate is presented when application for license is made. In most instances, then, a waiting period is required before the license is actually issued. The most common period of time specified is five days. However, this, too, varies with states.

Under certain circumstances that satisfy the court, the required advance notice can be reduced or entirely waived. The purpose of the advance notice is to prevent hasty, fraudulent, freak, drunken, or runaway marriages that cannot stand the light of public exposure. Seldom is it a hardship for normal people to let their intentions be known several days in advance.

The License

The law prohibits any officiant from marrying persons who have no license. Penalties may result for the one who illegally joins couples who have not received one.

The license is the keystone to the whole structure of marriage regulation by the state, for it is supposed to be the proof that the applicants have met all state requirements as to age, parental consent, dissolution of previous marriage, and physical and mental capacity, and have official sanction to wed.

In most states only one person need apply for the license, a few require both parties to appear, and in a few cases it is even possible for a third party to make the application. Some states require only the statement of one or both applicants that all the requirements have been met; others require one or both to give such testimony under oath; and a few require also the affidavit of a third party.

The officiant should promptly refuse to marry a couple if there is the slightest evidence of irregularity, or until such can be cleared to his satisfaction.

It is extremely important that the marriage license, signed by the officiant and witnesses (two required in most states), be returned to the issuing office, for it constitutes a permanent record. The officiant is responsible for making the return, and usually there is a penalty if the delay is beyond a certain length of time—that is, three days in many states.

Where Must the Wedding Be Held?

In most states, the marriage must be performed in the county of the office issuing the license. In all states, it must be performed within the state where the license is issued. If a marriage is legal in the state where it is performed, it is legal everywhere, except when it is void by express statutes forbidding such marriages—such as consanguinity. This is true of marriages in other countries as well, except when there is conflict with our marriage statutes, or when the persons are not legally free to marry.

Who May Marry?

What Are the Legal Ages for Marriage— With or Without Consent?

The most common minimum legal age for girls to marry with parental consent is sixteen; without parental consent it is eighteen. For boys, the legal age is eighteen with parental consent, and twenty-one without. However, the age requirements do vary slightly from state to state, as indicated later in this chapter.

What Are the Laws Regarding Marrying Relatives

In all states, marriage is prohibited between sister and brother, mother and son, father and daughter, grandmother and grandson, grandfather and granddaughter, uncle and niece, aunt and nephew.

For the marrying of other relatives, there is no legal uniformity. In twenty-nine jurisdictions, first cousins may not marry. Nine states prohibit marriage to a grandniece (or grandnephew), and six states forbid marriage to a first cousin once removed. Many states also extend prohibitions to relatives by half-blood (half-brothers and sisters, half-cousins, and so on).

Also, there are marriage prohibitions between persons who, though not related by blood, have a close affinity by marriage. The most common such prohibition (in twenty-three states) is that against marriage between stepparents and stepchildren. Twenty states forbid the marriage of father and daughter-in-law or of mother and son-in-law; eighteen prohibit a man from marrying his wife's granddaughter, even though sprung from a previous marriage; twelve will not allow a man to marry his wife's mother or a woman her husband's father.

What Other Conditions Prohibit Marriage?

All states have laws related to the marriage of the insane, feebleminded, and mentally incapable, which are to a considerable extent inheritable. Not all states positively forbid such marriages however. Seventeen states prohibit the marriage of epileptics, seven of them making exceptions in cases where the woman involved is over forty-five years of age. Two states permit hereditary epileptics to marry after they have been sterilized by an operation.

Three states prohibit the marriage of persons having infectious tuberculosis, and two forbid a person having any communicable disease to marry. Twenty-six states forbid marriages where either party has syphilis or gonorrhea.

Who Is Considered Married?

Is Common-law Marriage Legal?

When a man and woman make an agreement that they are husband and wife, live together in this relationship, and represent it as a marriage before their friends and the public in general, they are parties to common-law marriage. In most states, such receives no valid recognition by the law. The states that do recognize common-law marriages as legal are: Alabama; Colorado; District of Columbia; Florida (if entered into before January 1, 1968); Georgia; Idaho; Illinois (if entered into before June 30, 1905); Indiana (if entered into before June, 1958); Iowa; Kansas (both parties guilty of misdemeanor); Michigan (if entered into before January 1, 1957); Minnesota (if entered into before April 16, 1941); Mississippi (if entered into before April 5, 1956); Montana; Nebraska (if entered into before 1923); Nevada (if entered into before March 29, 1943); New Jersey (if entered into before December 1, 1939); New York (if entered into before April 29, 1933); Ohio; Oklahoma; Pennsylvania; Rhode Island; South Carolina; South Dakota (if entered into before July 1, 1959); Texas; Wisconsin (if entered into before 1917).

When Can a Marriage Be Annulled?

Divorce terminates marriages that have been legally recognized, whereas annulment is a judicial declaration that no valid marriage ever existed between the parties in question. All states provide for annulment, the most common grounds being: not of age, mental incapacity, force or duress, consanguinity or affinity, miscegenation, and fraud of some kind, such as concealment of insanity, impotency, conviction of a felony, and prior undissolved marriage.

The average duration of marriages ending in annulment is very short (one-third last less than one year).

Making a Marriage Official

Besides getting a marriage license, a bride and groom must see to it that proof of their marriage is put on file with the county clerk. After the ceremony, the clergyman or state official usually mails the marriage license to the county clerk for filing.

The Rights and Duties of Husbands and Wives

When major domestic difficulties arise, the law may step in to resolve them. A husband and wife are expected to live in the same house; under normal circumstances the husband has the legal right to decide where they shall live. If the husband's firm assigns him to a work in another part of the world, his wife has a legal duty to accompany him. If she refuses, she is guilty of desertion. The law is not inflexible: If her refusal is based upon health, she need not accompany her husband. A husband may not force his wife to a totally alien environment; in such a case he may be the one charged with desertion.

Wherever the home is located, the wife is the undisputed head. The husband cannot move his mother in and allow her to dominate the household. If she does, the wife can move out without a charge of desertion. The husband has no legal right to compel his wife to move in with his parents.

Supporting the Wife

The most fundamental law governing marriage is that a husband must support his wife. He must provide food, clothing, shelter, and medical care. If a husband refuses to do so and is not destitute himself, the wife may get a court order to force him to furnish these essentials.[1]

The courts conclude that however wealthy the husband, he is not required to give his wife a luxurious existence, so long as the comforts he does provide are in keeping with the mode of life he has chosen.

The Right of Consortium

Between husband and wife there is no more important mutually enjoyed legal right than consortium, the conjugal relation of husband and wife. It gives one spouse the right to "the person, affection, society and assistance" of the other spouse.

A husband is as legally entitled to the domestic services of his wife as he is to her "affection and person." The husband need not pay her for performing the household tasks.

A husband may institute legal proceedings against any third party who, even inadvertently, deprives him of his wife's company and services. The law also recognizes the wife's equal right in this regard.

Marriage Laws[2]

All states require that persons be at least a certain minimum age in order to obtain a marriage license. Persons below that age—18 in most states, must usually have the consent of their parents under oath before a judge or a witness. Court approval may also be required. In all states, it is illegal for a man to marry his sister, half-sister, mother, daughter, granddaughter, grandmother, great-grandmother, aunt, or neice. A woman may not marry her brother, half-brother, father, son, grandson, grandfather, great-

	At what age may you legally be married?				What other relatives are you prohibited from marrying?[1]
	With parental consent		Without parental consent		
	Male	Female	Male	Female	
ALABAMA	14	14	18	18	Stepparent, stepchild, son-in-law, daughter-in-law
ALASKA	16	16	18	18	——
ARIZONA	16[g]	16	18	18	First cousin
ARKANSAS	17	16[h]	21	18	First cousin
CALIFORNIA	18[g]	18	18	18	——
COLORADO	16	16	18	18	——
CONNECTICUT	16	16[j]	18	18	Stepparent, stepchild
DELAWARE	18	16[k]	18	18	First cousin
DISTRICT OF COLUMBIA	16	16	18	18	Stepparent, stepchild, stepgrandparent, father-in-law, mother-in-law, son-in-law, daughter-in-law, spouse's grandparent or grandchild, spouse of grandparent or grandchild

grandfather, uncle, or nephew. Many states also prohibit marriages between more distant relatives. Every state must recognize a common-law marriage that has been entered into in another state and is considered valid in that state. These and other state laws regulating marriage are summarized below.

Is a blood test required to obtain a license?	What is the waiting period between application and issue of a license?	How soon after issue of license may you marry?	How long is license valid after issuance?	Are common-law marriages recognized?
Yes	None	Immediately	30 days	Yes
Yes	3 days	Immediately	90 days	No
Yes	None	Immediately	No statutory provision	No
Yes	3 days	Immediately	No statutory provision	No
Yes	None	Immediately	90 days	No
Yes	None	Immediately	30 days	Yes
Yes	4 days	Immediately	65 days	No
Yes	None	1 day[2]	30 days	No
Yes	3 days	Immediately	No statutory provision	Yes

	At what age may you legally be married?				What other relatives are you prohibited from marrying?[1]
	With parental consent		Without parental consent		
	Male	Female	Male	Female	
FLORIDA	16	16	18	18	——
GEORGIA	Under 16[g]	Under 16[g]	18	18	Stepparent, stepchild, stepgrand-parent, stepgrandchild, father-in-law, mother-in-law, son-in-law, daughter-in-law
HAWAII	16	16	18	18	——
IDAHO	16	16	18	18	First cousin
ILLINOIS[a]	16	16	18	18	First cousin
INDIANA	17[k]	17[k]	18	18	First cousin
IOWA	[k]	[k]	18	18	First cousin, stepparent, stepchild, father-in-law, mother-in-law, son-in-law, daughter-in-law, spouse of grandchild

48

Is a blood test required to obtain a license?	What is the waiting period between application and issue of a license?	How soon after issue of license may you marry?	How long is license valid after issuance?	Are common-law marriages recognized?
Yes	3 days	Immediately	30 days	No, unless entered into before Jan. 1, 1968
Yes	None[k]	Immediately	30 days	Yes
Yes	None	Immediately	30 days	No
Yes	3 days if either is under 18; otherwise, none	Immediately	No statutory provision	Yes
Yes	None	1 day	60 days	No, unless entered into before June 30, 1905
Yes	3 days	Immediately	60 days	No, unless entered into before 1958
Yes	3 days	Immediately	20 days	Yes

| | At what age may you legally be married? | | | | What other relatives are you prohibited from marrying?[1] |
| | With parental consent | | Without parental consent | | |
	Male	Female	Male	Female	
KANSAS	14	12	18	18	First cousin
KENTUCKY	No statutory provision[k]	No statutory provision[k]	18	18	First cousin, first cousin once removed
LOUISIANA	18[k]	16[h]	18	16	First cousin
MAINE	16[h]	16[h]	18	18	Stepparent, stepchild, father-in-law, mother-in-law, son-in-law, daughter-in-law, spouse's grandparent or grandchild, spouse of grandparent or grandchild
MARYLAND	16	16	18	18	Stepparent, stepchild, father-in-law, mother-in-law, son-in-law, daughter-in-law, spouse's grandparent or grandchild, spouse of grandparent or grandchild
MASSACHUSETTS	No statutory provision[k]	No statutory provision[k]	18	18	Stepparent, stepchild, stepgrandparent, father-in-law, mother-in-law, son-in-law, daughter-in-law

	Is a blood test required to obtain a license?	What is the waiting period between application and issue of a license?	How soon after issue of license may you marry?	How long is license valid after issuance?	Are common-law marriages recognized?
	Yes	3 days	Immediately	No statutory provision	Yes, but parties guilty of misdemeanor
	Yes	3 days	Immediately	30 days	No
	Yes	None	3 days	30 days	No
	No	5 days	Immediately	60 days	No
	No	2 days	Immediately	6 months	No
	Yes	3 days	Immediately	60 days	No

| | At what age may you legally be married? | | | | What other relatives are you prohibited from marrying?[1] |
| | With parental consent | | Without parental consent | | |
	Male	Female	Male	Female	
MICHIGAN[a]	16	16	18	18	First cousin
MINNESOTA	16[e]	16[e]	18	18	First cousin
MISSISSIPPI	17[L,3]	15[L,3]	21	21	First cousin, stepparent, stepchild, father-in-law, mother-in-law, son-in-law, daughter-in-law
MISSOURI	15	15	18	18	First cousin
MONTANA	15	15	18	18	First cousin
NEBRASKA	17	17	18	18	First cousin
NEVADA	16	16	18	18	First cousin
NEW HAMPSHIRE[a]	14[e]	13[e]	18	18	First cousin, stepparent, son-in-law, daughter-in-law
NEW JERSEY[a]	[g]	12	18	18	——

Is a blood test required to obtain a license?	What is the waiting period between application and issue of a license?	How soon after issue of license may you marry?	How long is license valid after issuance?	Are common-law marriages recognized?
Yes	3 days	Immediately	33 days	No, unless entered into before Jan. 1, 1957
No	5 days	Immediately	6 months	No, unless entered into before Apr. 16, 1941
Yes	3 days if 1 person is under 21	Immediately	No statutory provision	No, unless entered into before Apr. 5, 1956
Yes	3 days	Immediately	No statutory provision	No, unless entered into before Mar. 31, 1921
Yes	None	3 days	180 days	Yes
Yes	2 days	Immediately	No statutory provision	No, unless entered into before 1923
No	None	Immediately	No statutory provision	No, unless entered into before Mar. 29, 1943
Yes	5 days	Immediately	90 days	No
Yes	3 days	Immediately	30 days	No, unless entered into before Dec. 1, 1939

	At what age may you legally be married?				What other relatives are you prohibited from marrying?[1]
	With parental consent		Without parental consent		
	Male	Female	Male	Female	
NEW MEXICO	16	16	18	18	——
NEW YORK	16	14[c]	18	18	——
NORTH CAROLINA[a]	16	16	18	18	Double first cousin
NORTH DAKOTA[a]	16	16	18	18	First cousin
OHIO	18	16	18	18	First cousin
OKLAHOMA	16	16	18	18	First cousin
OREGON	17	17	18	18	First cousin
PENNSYLVANIA	16	16	18	18	First cousin, stepparent, stepchild, son-in-law, daughter-in-law
RHODE ISLAND[a,b]	14	12	18	18	Stepchild, father-in-law, mother-in-law, spouse's grandparent or grandchild
SOUTH CAROLINA	14	12	18	18	Stepparent, stepchild, father-in-law, mother-in-law, son-in-law, daughter-in-law, spouse's grandparent or grandchild, spouse of grandparent or grandchild

Is a blood test required to obtain a license?	What is the waiting period between application and issue of a license?	How soon after issue of license may you marry?	How long is license valid after issuance?	Are common-law marriages recognized?
Yes	None	Immediately	No statutory provision	No
Yes	None	1 day[f]	60 days	No, unless entered into before Apr. 29, 1933
Yes[4]	None	Immediately	No statutory provision	No
Yes	None	Immediately	60 days	No
Yes	5 days	Immediately	60 days	Yes
Yes	None	Immediately	30 days	Yes
Yes	3 days	Immediately	30 days after blood test	No
Yes	3 days	Immediately	60 days	Yes
Yes	None[5]	Immediately	3 months	Yes
No	24 hrs.	Immediately	No statutory provision	Yes

| | At what age may you legally be married? | | | | What other relatives are you prohibited from marrying?[1] |
| | With parental consent | | Without parental consent | | |
	Male	Female	Male	Female	
SOUTH DAKOTA	16	16	18	18	First cousin, stepparent, stepchild
TENNESSEE	16	16	18	18	Stepparent, stepchild, stepgrandchild, grandnephew, grandniece
TEXAS	14[k]	14[k]	18	18	——
UTAH[a]	14	14	18	18	First cousin
VERMONT[a]	16	16	18	18	——
VIRGINIA[a]	16	16	18	18	——
WASHINGTON	17	17	18	18	First cousin
WEST VIRGINIA	16	16	18	18	First cousin, double cousin
WISCONSIN	16	16	18	18	First cousin, unless female 55 years or older
WYOMING	16	16	19	19	First cousin

[1] Besides siblings, parents, children, grandchildren, grandparents, great-grandparents, uncles, aunts, nieces, and nephews.

[2] But there is a 4-day waiting period if both parties are nonresidents.

[3] There is no statutory minimum age limit; both parental consent and court order are required.

[4] A physical examination showing freedom from uncontrolled epilepsy, tuberculosis, idiocy, and insanity is also required.

[5] But there is a 5-day waiting period for female nonresidents.

Is a blood test required to obtain a license?	What is the waiting period between application and issue of a license?	How soon after issue of license may you marry?	How long is license valid after issuance?	Are common-law marriages recognized?
Yes	None	Immediately	20 days	No, unless entered into before July 1, 1959
Yes	3 days if either is under 18	Immediately	30 days	No
No	None	Immediately	21 days after medical examination	Yes
No	None	Immediately	30 days	No
Yes	None	5 days from application of license	60 days	No
Yes	None	Immediately	60 days	No
d	3 days	Immediately	30 days	No
Yes	3 days	Immediately	60 days	No
Yes	5 days	Immediately	30 days	No, unless entered into before 1917
Yes	None	Immediately	No statutory provision	No

Many states have additional special requirements; contact individual state. (a) Special laws applicable to nonresidents. (b) Special laws applicable to those under 21 years; Ala., bond required if male is under 18, female under 18. (c) 24 hours if one or both parties resident of state; 96 hours if both parties are non-residents. (d) None, but both must file affidavit. (e) Parental consent plus court's consent required. (f) Marriage may not be solemnized within 10 days from date of blood test. (g) Statute provides for obtaining license with parental or court consent with no state minimum age. (h) Under 16, with parental and court consent. (i) If either under 18, wait 3 full days. (j) If under stated age, court consent required. (k) If under 18, parental and/or court consent required. (l) Both parents' consent required for men age 17, women age 15; one parent's consent required for men 18–20 years, women ages 16–20 years.

Canadian Marriage Information[3]

Source: Compiled from information provided by the various provincial government departments and agencies concerned.

Marriageable age, by provinces, for both males and females with and without consent of parents or guardians. In some provinces, the court has authority, given special circumstances, to marry young couples below the minimum age. Most provinces waive the blood test requirement and the waiting period varies across the provinces.

Province	With consent		Without consent		Blood test		Wait for license	Wait after license
	Men	Women	Men	Women	Required	other province Accepted		
Newfoundland	16	16	19	19	None	None	4 days	4 days
Prince Edward Island .	16	16	18	18	Yes	Yes	5 days	None
Nova Scotia	(1)	(1)	19	19	None	None	5 days	None
New Brunswick	16	14	18	18	None	None	5 days	None
Quebec	14	12	18	18	None	—	5 days	None
Ontario	16	16	18	18	None	—	None[2]	None
Manitoba	16	16	18	18	Yes	Yes	None	3 days
Saskatchewan	15	15	18	18	Yes	Yes	5 days	24 hours
Alberta	16[8]	16[8]	18	18	Yes[3]	Yes[4]	None[5]	24 hours
British Columbia	16[6]	16[6]	19	19	None	None	2 days[7]	None
Yukon Territory	15	15	19	19	None	None	None	24 hours
Northwest Territories .	15	15[9]	19	19	None	Yes	None	None

(1) There is no statutory minimum age in the province. Anyone under the age of 19 years must have consent for marriage and no person under the age of 16 may be married without authorization of a Family Court judge and in addition must have the necessary consent of the parent or guardian. (2) Special requirements applicable to nonresidents. (3) Applies only to applicants under 60 years of age. (4) This is upon filing of negative lab report indicating blood test was taken within 14 days preceding date of application for license. (5) Exception where consent is required by mail; depending receipt of divorce documents, etc. (6) Persons under 16 years of age (no minimum age specified) may also be married if they have obtained, in addition to the usual consent from parents or guardian, an order from a judge of the Supreme or County Court in this province. (7) Including day of application, e.g., a license applied for on a Monday cannot be issued until Wednesday. (8) Under 16 allowed if pregnant or the mother of a living child. (9) Under 15 allowed if pregnant or with the written permission of the Commissioner of the NWT.

The Duties and Rights of a Working Wife

A husband has no claim on money his wife earns from outside-the-home employment. Under the law the paycheck belongs to her, to spend or save as she wishes.

A husband who owns a business can ask his wife to work for him without salary. However, he would be far wiser to pay her a salary. Should she be injured while working, unless she were a salaried employee, she could not collect disability payments under the Workmen's Compensation Act.

The Wife's Property

A wife has a right to own and control her own property acquired before marriage. In most states a woman also owns outright any property she acquires while married. However, in community-property states, all mutually acquired property belongs equally to husband and wife. A wife has the right "to make contracts, engage in business, be employed, keep outside earnings, and legal independence."[4] She can sue or be sued on her own. A husband is not liable for damage judgments against his wife, unless the harm done was partly his fault.

A wife's property remains beyond her husband's creditors. For this reason some husbands with large businesses vulnerable to damage suits transfer substantial family assets to their wives' ownership.

"A wife may convey her own property in any way she chooses, that is, she can sell it, leave it in a will, or give it to her children, family, friends, or charitable institutions."[5] She cannot turn it temporarily over to her husband and be sure of getting it back if he dies, unless she retains convincing evidence.

The Right Not to Have Children

"In 1965 the Supreme Court ruled that no state had the right to tell husbands and wives that they could not use artificial contraceptive devices; in every state, married people can now buy contraceptives, use them and obtain advice from doctors and clinics on the most suitable kinds"[6] without risking the danger of violating the law.

On January 22, 1973, the Supreme Court, in the landmark cases of *Roe* v. *Wade* and *Doe* v. *Balton,* held that a woman, after counsel with her doctor, has a constitutional right to make a decision to have an abortion. The medical definition of abortion is the termination of pregnancy prior to the stage of viability. She has the right to choose to continue a pregnancy or to end it.

The law states that abortion procedures must be performed by licensed physicians. In the first three months, abortion may be performed in a clinic or a doctor's office. After three months, special conditions may be imposed by certain states to protect and preserve the health of the woman. In the third trimester the state can regulate or prohibit all abortions except those necessary to protect a woman's life or health.[7]

"The ruling applies equally to all women, married and unmarried, adults and minors."[8]

Controversy still rages. Antiabortion activists have campaigned in Congress and throughout the states to reverse that decision by passing a constitutional amendment. Church bodies remain divided on the issue.

At present the legal situation is uniform: The law affirms the right of the woman to make her own decision regarding the continuation or termination of pregnancy.

Dissolving a Marriage

A couple can be legally parted in three ways: through annulment, legal separation, and divorce.

Annulment

An annulment is a court decision saying that some obstacle made the marriage invalid from the start. The law distinguishes two kinds of obstacles.

An incestuous marriage or a marriage contracted by a person who is already married automatically voids a marriage.

The following obstacles also form the basis of annulment:

UNDERAGE: "If either husband or wife was below the age for marriage set by law in their state, parents may bring legal action on behalf of their minor child."[9]

SEXUAL IMPOTENCE: "If either partner proves physically or psychologically incapable of intercourse from the beginning of the marriage, it can be annulled."[10]

LACK OF TRUE CONSENT: The validity of a marriage can be questioned if a couple gets married flippantly, with no real intention of a lasting relationship, if either is of unsound mind, or if either is married under duress.

FRAUD: Annulments have been granted for concealment of serious illness, mental disorder, important information about a previous marriage, pregnancy of a bride by a man other than her husband, lying by either partner about a desire to have children.[11]

Legal Separations

When annulment is not possible, a divorce can end marriage. Couples who decide that they can no longer live together but who shy away from divorce may resort to the halfway step of a judicial separation. The proceeding requires one or both parties to appear in court, to negotiate the agreement; then they receive a decree of "divorce from bed and board."[11]

Separation does not entirely free a couple from responsibility of marriage. The husband is still obligated to support his wife and children and both husband and wife are barred from engaging in adulterous conduct, a difficult agreement to enforce.

If the couple reconciles after a voluntary separation, they simply tear up their agreement to live apart. In the case of a judicial separation, the court must be petitioned to revoke the agreement.

Divorce

The state laws provide a variety of grounds for legal divorce: physical cruelty, where one spouse inflicts bodily harm upon the other; mental cruelty, where one spouse persistently, with malicious intent, insults, abuses, or humiliates the other, making the marriage intolerable. Almost all states grant divorce for adultery, but only three recognize attempted murder of a spouse as grounds. Most states have adopted no-fault grounds for divorce; in such case a spouse no longer must prove that the other has committed a marital wrong.

There are four ways that divorce action can be stopped:

CONDONATION: If one has committed adultery but the spouse nevertheless allows the offender back home and they have intercourse, the forgiveness rules out the divorce for adultery suit.

CONNIVANCE: Where one spouse deliberately plots to create grounds for divorce against the other, a divorce will not be granted.

RECRIMINATION: If a husband and wife are equally guilty of misbehavior, neither can get a divorce.

COLLUSION: A couple conspiring to proffer false evidence will not receive a divorce.

Migratory Divorce

Some people become impatient with divorce proceedings so seek a quick release from unhappy marriages by obtaining migratory divorces in other countries or other states. Nevada, Idaho, Arkansas, South Dakota, and Wyoming have relaxed divorce laws, thus luring incoming divorce seekers. Residency requirements are six weeks in Nevada and Idaho, only sixty days in Wyoming and Arkansas, and none in South Dakota. The judge will usually hand down the divorce decree as soon as the residency requirements have been fulfilled. If the spouse does not consent to the divorce, but does not migrate to contest it, the judge gives the *ex parte* decree to the one appearing. A one-sided divorce bears the danger that such a decree may prove worthless if challenged in a court in the home state. If the spouse does cooperate, he or she signs an agreement that he or she recognizes and submits to the migratory divorce and will not later move to invalidate the decree.

Grounds for Divorce in Canada[12]

Source: Government of Canada Divorce Act
The grounds for divorce in Canada are the same for all the provinces and its territories. There are two categories of offense.

A. Marital Offense:
Adultery
Sodomy
Bestiality
Rape
Homosexual act
Subsequent marriage
Physical cruelty
Mental cruelty

B. Marriage breakdown by reason of:
Imprisonment for aggregate period of not less than 3 years
Imprisonment for not less than 2 years on sentence of death or sentence of 10 years or more
Addiction to alcohol
Addiction to narcotics
Whereabouts of spouse unknown
Non-consummation
Separation for not less than 3 years
Desertion by petitioner for not less than 5 years

Residence time: Domicile in Canada. Time between interlocutory and final decree: normally 3 months before final can be applied for.

Chapter Four

The Spiritual Significance of the Wedding Service

There is a significant trend in our culture toward the renewed importance of marriage and the wedding ceremony.

A decade ago many young couples were questioning, "Why is a ceremony necessary? We are just as much married in our hearts whether or not we have a wedding service. The certificate is just a piece of paper. We will simply live together without marriage."

The latest statistics indicate that beginning in 1976 marriages have increased in the United States. In 1982 there were 2 percent more marriages and nearly 4 percent less divorces than in 1981, according to the National Center for Health Statistics, United States Department of Health and Human Services.

Increasingly, ceremonies are felt important in life to make public what we feel in our hearts, to openly declare our commitments, and to celebrate significant occasions with our families and friends. The wedding ceremony is perhaps the most meaningful and widely observed ritual of all.

Apparently couples are recognizing more and more that two people living together without marriage have no legal obligations to one another.

The Importance of the Ceremony

The minister begins the wedding service with such words as: "Dearly beloved, we are gathered together here in the presence of God to join this man and this woman in holy matrimony, an estate instituted by God, regulated by His commandments, and to be held in honor among all men." The first fact of Christian marriage is that it is undertaken in the presence of God. It is holy matrimony, instituted *by God,* not by man. By marrying in a church, the bride and groom affirm that God joins them together. Central attention is not focused on the bride, but on God, the One "altogether lovely." Hence, marriage "is not to be entered into unadvisably or lightly, but reverently, discreetly, soberly, and in the fear of God." In Christian marriage, it is God who matters most of all. The relationship is to be regulated by His commandments.

Most ceremonies include such words as: "Marriage is to be held in honor among all men," or "If any of you know cause, or just impediment, why these two persons should not be joined in holy matrimony, you are to declare it." One of the main features of the wedding service in the Judaic and Christian tradition is its public character.[1] Though marriage is intensely personal and intimate, it is never a completely private matter. Society is involved "for better or for worse"; family traditions and reputations are implicated. "Who giveth this woman to be joined to this man?"—When the father has identified himself and gives the family's public approval and the daughter withdraws her hand, the way is open for the new relationship to be established. Marriage is a highly pleasurable undertaking, but it is not primarily a device designed to provide personal pleasures for two people.

The union is likely to produce children, who may be either a burden or a strength to the community. Hence, each marriage is of concern to all. The family is a fundamental unit of society, for it is the medium to propagate the human race, to satisfy emotional needs in beneficial ways, and to perpetuate religious experience. The community has a stake in every new union. The "secret" marriage is a contradiction in terms, and a "quickie" marriage indicates failure to appreciate this public character. This public significance of marriage has led to the establishment of laws whereby the marriage intention is acknowledged openly prior to the solemnizing of it.

The religious wedding service, in essence, is the giving of public approval to the union by the family, the church, and the community. Marriage, therefore, is not to be entered into lightly, but "reverently, discreetly, and soberly" and in the presence of those whose approbation and blessing the couple seek.

Furthermore, the religious wedding service is the recognition before God that marriage is a lifelong commitment. It is not a mere contract or bargain that has certain contingencies and escape clauses. The two participants in marriage pledge themselves "for better, for worse; for richer, for poorer; in sickness and in health." It frankly recognizes in advance the possibilities of economic difficulties, illness, sterility, and other dangers and pitfalls. Nonetheless, marriage is not conceived as a temporary arrangement, to be honored only so long as relationships are mutually pleasant; rather, it is a pledge to be respected "so long as we both shall live."

Hence, it is intrinsically a relationship of mutually corresponding obligations. The ceremony includes such thoughts as: "Our Lord through his apostles has instructed those who enter this relation to cherish a mutual esteem and love; to bear with each other's infirmities and weaknesses; to comfort each other in sickness, trouble, and sorrow; in honesty and industry to provide for each other and for their household in temporal things; to pray for and encourage each other in the things that pertain to God; and to live together as heirs of his grace." When a minister says to the man and woman before him, "I therefore require and charge you both," he does not use empty phrases.

Marriage is an arrangement in which each partner gives *all* that he has: "with all my worldly goods I thee endow." A marriage is not a marriage at all if it is partial or entered into with fingers crossed or with the idea that it is but a temporary trial that can be dissolved at the divorce court if unsatisfactory. There must be a mutual outpouring of unlimited love. A truly married person is more interested in his mate's happiness than in his own. The wedding is the sacred service during which a man and a woman make these vows of lifelong fidelity.

Since marriage is a venture of faith, the wedding ceremony is, in reality, the couple's acceptance of the church's faith.[2] The couple speak for themselves while they stand at the foot of the chancel steps. The minister asks the groom, and then the bride: "Will you love, comfort, honor, and keep (him or her) in sickness and in health; and forsaking all others, keep yourself only unto (him or her) so long as you both shall live?" Each responds, "I will." Thus, the gulf is spanned between the faith of the church and the faith of the persons who come to the church to be married. The attitude of the church toward marriage is that it is a holy relationship. It is a life of loving, comforting, honoring, and keeping; there is no wavering in sickness or in health; and from the day of marriage to the day of death, no other man or woman shall invade the sacred precincts of sexual union. For nineteen centuries this has also been the faith of the church. With the speaking of the words "I will," the faith of the church is accepted by the couple; this is the kind of relationship they intend their marriage to be.

The man and the woman ascend the chancel steps to the altar to make their promises to one another. Looking into each other's eyes, they repeat the words that bind their lives together for the rest of their days on earth: "I, John, take thee, Mary, to be my wedded wife, to have and to hold, from this day forward . . . till death do us part." To bring to remembrance the wedding day and to seal the promises, ring symbols are exchanged, "in token and pledge of constant faith and abiding love." The wedding ceremony is the public acceptance of the bond which limits free expression. The possibility of dating or making love with others is ruled out by virtue of the wedding bond. The pledge of fidelity and the dedication to faithfulness are implied in the ring exchange. Marriage is not compatible with absolute freedom, yet the person who binds himself to one life mate finds the highest level of freedom.

The sacredness of the wedding ring was understood by Carl Sandburg's mother. Said he, "Mama's wedding ring was never lost—was always on that finger, placed there with pledges years ago. It was a sign and seal of something that ran deep and held fast between the two of them. They had chosen each other as partners. . . ." So should it be for all who are joined in holy matrimony.

Speaking as an agent of the living God and as a representative of the whole community, the minister pronounces that the union is indeed a fact: "I pronounce that they are husband and wife. . . . What God, then, has joined together, let no man put asunder."

The basis of unity is the fact that in this bond two persons are joined together so as to become "one flesh." ". . . they are no longer two individuals: they are one flesh" (Matthew 19:6 NEB).

This unity of two in one flesh is not just biological, as it is for animals; rather, it also has spiritual and psychic qualities. Marriage brings into play, not just two biological beings, but two personalities. The dialogue is of the spirit; the kiss is of the soul; the spirit's intensity is echoed by the flesh.

Nowhere in Scripture is marriage discussed in terms of sex; instead it is discussed in terms of knowledge. The closest union that exists between anything in the universe and man himself is possible only through knowledge. When man knows a flower or a tree, he "possesses" these objects within his mind.

Similarly, marriage involves the mind, soul, heart, and will, as well as the reproductive organs. It is one of the closest unions possible, more personal than carnal. The union is something more than the physical union of the two sexes; the union is psychosomatic, affecting the whole person, body and soul. In the moment of "knowing," each partner receives a gift which neither ever knew before. Henceforth, the woman can never return to her virginity; the man can never return to ignorance. Something happens in oneness; and from that oneness comes fidelity.

The ceremony ends, and a great new life begins, hallowed in the spirit of prayer: "The Lord bless, preserve, and keep you; the Lord mercifully with his favor look upon you, and fill you with all spiritual benediction and grace; that you may so live together in this life that in the world to come you may have life everlasting."

Chapter Five

The Details of Wedding Planning

The Types of Weddings

One of the first decisions is to choose the type of wedding wanted. The types are:

1. The ultraformal wedding is usually held in the church, with six to twelve bridal attendants and an equal number of groomsmen. All dress is meticulously formal. In the eastern part of the United States such a wedding is scheduled at noon, four, or four-thirty in the afternoon. In the South, Midwest, and West it takes place in the evening or late afternoon.
2. The formal wedding is not quite as sophisticated and perfect as the ultraformal. There are a large number of bridal attendants and a like number of male attendants. The formal wedding usually takes place in the church, but may be in a home, a garden, hotel or club. Attire is formal, with long dresses for all bridal attendants and mothers and tuxedos for male participants.
3. The semiformal wedding may be held in the church sanctuary or chapel, in the home or garden, at a hotel or a club. Any time in the afternoon or evening is proper, except the semiformal Roman Catholic wedding is held in the morning. There are usually only two or three female attendants and as many male attendants.

69

The wedding is usually smaller than the formal wedding. The bride wears a floor-length gown and her attendants floor or ballerina length. The groom and male attendants may wear dinner jackets after six o'clock; otherwise dark blue suits with midnight blue or black bow ties.

4. The informal wedding may be held in the church sanctuary, chapel, parsonage, in a home, garden, hotel, or club. It may be scheduled anytime during the day, but not usually in the evening. Engraved invitations are not generally used. Guests are invited verbally or by handwritten notes. There are no formal attendants, but two legal witnesses are needed to sign the certificates so are usually considered the best man and bridesmaid. Decorations are optional; if chosen, they are very simple. There is no music, hence no processional. There are no ushers, hence there is no formal seating of guests or mothers.

Military Wedding

A military wedding may be held when the groom is a commissioned officer or a reserve officer on active duty. Military weddings are usually ultraformal or formal. They are never informal. Most military weddings are held in the church sanctuary. No boutonnieres or flowers are worn with a military uniform. Medals may be worn. The groom wears regulation summer or winter dress uniform, as do his attendants, the type prescribed by his particular branch of service. The groom's attendants are fellow officers. If there is a mixture of civilian attendants, they are paired together as are the officers in the procession.

If there is to be an arch of swords or sabres, it takes place outside the church; only officers take part. Only the bride and groom pass under the arch.

The Officiating Minister

People should be married by their own minister, if at all possible, in order that there may be a permanent relationship

Wedding Guide[1]

	Formal	Semiformal	Informal
Bride's dress	Long white gown, train, veil optional	Long white gown, veil optional	White or pastel cocktail dress or suit or afternoon dress (sometimes, very simple long gown)
Bridesmaids' dresses	Long or according to current style	Long or according to current style	Same type of dress as worn by bride
Dress of groom and his attendants	Cutaway or tailcoat	Sack coat or tuxedo	Dark business suit or jacket
Bride's attendants	Maid or matron of honor, 4–10 bridesmaids, flower girl, ring bearer (optional)	Maid or matron of honor, 2–6 bridesmaids, flower girl, ring bearer (optional)	Maid or matron of honor, 1 or 2 children (optional)
Groom's attendants	Best man; 1 usher for every 50 guests, or same number as bridesmaids	Best man; 1 usher for every 50 guests, or same number as bridesmaids	Best man; 1 usher if necessary to seat guests
Location of ceremony	Church, synagogue, or large home or garden	Church, synagogue, chapel, hotel, club, home, garden	Chapel, rectory, justice of the peace, home, garden
Location of reception	Club, hotel, garden, or large home	Club, restaurant, hotel, garden, home	Church parlor, home, restaurant
Number of guests	200 or more	75 to 200	75 or under
Provider of service at reception	Caterer at home, or club or hotel facilities	Caterer at home, or club or hotel facilities	Caterer, friends and relatives, or restaurant
Food	Sit-down or semi-buffet (tables provided for bridal party, parents, and guests); hot meal served; wedding cake	Buffet (bridal party and parents may have tables); cocktail buffet food, sandwiches, cold cuts, snacks, wedding cake	Stand-up buffet or 1 table for all guests; may be a meal or snacks and wedding cake
Invitations and announcements	Engraved	Engraved	Handwritten or telephoned invitations; engraved announcements

Wedding Guide[1] (continued)

	Formal	Semiformal	Informal
Decorations and accessories	Elaborate flowers for church, canopy to church, aisle carpet, pew ribbons, limousines for bridal party, groom's cake (given to guests in boxes), engraved matchbooks or napkins as mementos, rose petals or confetti	Flowers for church, aisle carpet, pew ribbons, rose petals (other items optional)	Flowers for altar, rose petals
Music	Organ at church (choir or soloist optional); orchestra for dancing at reception	Organ at church (choir or soloist optional); strolling musician, small orchestra, or records for reception; dancing optional	Organ at church; records at reception optional

between the officiating minister and the family which he helps to bring into existence. When young people are married by an outsider, the occasion is robbed of some of the intimate values.

Generally, the bride's minister conducts the service because normally it is in her church. When held in the groom's hometown, the presiding minister may be the groom's pastor. On occasion, both ministers may be involved.

If the bride's or groom's father is a minister, he is usually accorded the privilege of performing the marriage of his child, usually with the church minister assisting.

If a relative of the bride or groom is a minister, he or she may be asked to assist.

It is a matter of ministerial ethics that a minister does not return to a former parish to perform pastoral duties or assume privileges. The rare occasion for acceptance of such participation may be on the condition that he is invited by the local minister to assist. It is quite easy for a minister to say to a family or a prospective bride who asks him to officiate in his former parish: "I am sorry. As much as I would like to participate, I cannot presume upon the privilege of the local minister. With his invitation, I might assist him in the service. You talk with him about it."

Often the church policy can strengthen this position and save the church's minister from much embarrassment by stating that "a staff member of the local church must be a part of all weddings held." Thus, the outside minister would have an assisting role only.

Place of the Wedding

Young people should be married in their own communities, so that parents, relatives, and friends may attend. If they come from different communities, the wedding is usually held in the bride's community. A marriage is of concern to all who are close to those who marry; the ceremony is made public because, in essence, it implies community approval.

Stunt weddings or obscure, sensational locations for weddings are to be discouraged, because they rob marriage of the intimate and sacred values.

It is strongly recommended that persons be married in the sanctuary or chapel of the church. The atmosphere would be one that lends reverence and a spirit of worship, thus contributing to the essential nature of marriage.

In some cases where the bride has been gone from home for several years, the wedding may take place where she or the groom live or work, or if in school, in that community.

The church sanctuary will accommodate a large wedding. The church chapel usually will be adequate for smaller weddings. Often a simple reception can also be accommodated in a social area of the church. All this will cost less than a hotel or club.

Home weddings are preferred by some because of the intimate family atmosphere. A makeshift altar with a wedding prie-dieu and candelabra are placed in front of a fireplace or in another proper location. Such plans usually sacrifice considerable orderliness, formality, and musical renderings. The reception is also held at the home. It is not necessary to try to seat every guest as long as there is seating for the older people.

On occasion, the location may be the rectory or parsonage, but only if the minister's wife is agreeable and very few guests are invited.

Sometimes weddings are held in a beautiful backyard, in a

flower-garden area, or in a special setting. Outdoor weddings may be beautiful, but the atmosphere of solemnity is not controlled and inclement weather is unpredictable. A quick-change alternative must be ready in that event.

Setting the Date

When making plans for the date of the wedding, many things need to be considered, including the season of the year, the time of the month, keeping in mind the bride's menstrual period, the day of the week, the time of day, and the availability of the minister and facilities.

June and August are popular summer months, especially with young people, because of completion of a school year on the one hand and because they are before the fall school term on the other hand. An August wedding allows the groom and bride to work during the summer. December has rivaled June as a most popular month. The period of Lent (forty days prior to Easter) is usually not chosen by Christians; winter is avoided because of cold weather.

Usually Christians do not choose Sundays or certain holy days for a wedding, nor do Orthodox Jews marry on the Sabbath (Friday sundown to Saturday sundown) or on the high holy days.

Informal Protestant weddings are seldom scheduled in the evening but may be any time during the morning or afternoon. Semiformal Protestant weddings may be at any time in the afternoon. The more formal weddings are usually in the evening with candlelight followed by a reception, a dinner, and dancing. Often however, the formal wedding is at high noon, afternoon, or six o'clock. The times of the day vary in different parts of the country.

Roman Catholic weddings are not held after sundown. Formal Catholic weddings with high mass are before noon. Semiformal Catholic weddings with low mass are early in the morning. Catholic weddings without the mass take place in the afternoon, with five o'clock as the preferred time.

Usually Saturday is the most popular wedding day, both afternoon and evening. More guests are able to attend. Remember that vacation periods and holidays increase the conflicts and the absences.

Checklist and Schedule for Bride and Groom

Four to Six Months Before Wedding

1. Arrange tentative date of wedding with clergyman. Fill in wedding form.
2. Plan premarital-counseling sessions with him, setting dates to meet.
3. Shop for engagement and wedding rings.
4. Borrow or buy at least one wedding planning book (they may vary in their advice, but they will provide good ideas). Research types of weddings and costs.

Twelfth Week Before Wedding

1. Bride and groom have final counseling session and begin to plan details.
2. Bride and mother meet with pastor to discuss type of wedding, to set final date, place, and time, to make reservations and deposits, and to discuss plans. Schedule minister, organists, and other staff.
3. Learn the policy of the church regarding costs, decorations, and so on.
4. Compare prices of local caterers, bakers, florists, photographers, rentals, and gowns.
5. Discuss budget and estimate costs. Make final decision as to type of wedding.

Eleventh Week Before Wedding

1. Bride selects her attendants and asks them to take part in the wedding. Groom does the same for his attendants.
2. Decide who will be invited to the reception.
3. List persons to whom wedding announcements should be sent.
4. Choose and order invitations if ultraformal, formal, or semiformal wedding is planned. For informal wedding, if invitations are to be sent, paper for handwritten invitations may be chosen.

5. Decide on announcements and order them (used for all types of weddings).
6. Meet with the caterer, if one is being used.
7. Bride should make an appointment with her gynecologist, for an examination to take place six to eight weeks before the wedding.

Tenth Week Before Wedding

1. Bride selects her gown or dress and those of her attendants. The groom selects his suit and those of his attendants.
2. Meet with insurance agent regarding insurance on rings, wedding gifts, and so on.
3. Help mothers choose gowns that will blend with each other's and the rest of the wedding party.

Ninth Week Before Wedding

1. Visit stores and compare furniture and appliances; choose housewares. Register for gifts.
2. Bride and attendants should order gowns or dresses. If gowns are to be made by those in the party, materials should be bought and work begun.
3. Rehearsal dinner plans, including date, time, place, and menu, should be completed.
4. Check with both families to finalize invitation list.
5. Address invitations, stamp envelopes, and hold for mailing. Informal wedding invitations may be written.

Eighth Week Before Wedding

1. Meet with musicians and go over the music for ceremony and reception.
2. Bride and groom select honeymoon location.
3. Make transportation and hotel reservations for honeymoon trip.
4. Check luggage required for honeymoon.
5. If trip is abroad, get birth certificates, order passports, get inoculations as necessary.

6. Make appointment with physician for fourth week before wedding.

Seventh Week Before Wedding

1. Place order with florist.
2. Choose a photographer and discuss wedding-day plans; make an appointment for newspaper photo.
3. Order printed favors for reception.
4. If any questions arise, check with minister.
5. Bride may plan luncheon or tea for bridesmaids.
6. Bride visits gynecologist.

Sixth Week Before Wedding

1. Choose and purchase attendants' gifts.
2. Bride and groom sit for wedding portrait for newspaper and prepare announcement.
3. Confirm flower orders.
4. Confirm reservations for honeymoon.
5. Mail invitations to wedding and rehearsal dinner. For informal weddings, call those who are to be invited if invitations are not to be sent. (For informal weddings, invitations may be sent later, but must be received at least two weeks before wedding.)

Fourth Week Before Wedding

1. Keep appointment with physician.
2. Have blood tests done.
3. Call attendants and make certain they will be able to be in the wedding party.
4. Arrange for transportation, maps, and lodging for out-of-town members of the wedding party.
5. Check with bridesmaids regarding gowns, shoes, and so on; get measurements from ushers and order rental suits and shoes.
6. Send local newspapers release of wedding plans.
7. Bride and groom have final fitting of clothes. Break in shoes.
8. Spend some quiet times together.

Third Week Before Wedding

1. Bride may have a luncheon or tea for bridesmaids.
2. Make hair appointments and so on.
3. Decide where bride, groom, and attendants will dress before wedding.
4. Move belongings to new home and arrange utilities, telephone, television, and mail.
5. Put someone in charge of gifts at reception.

Second Week Before Wedding

1. Get license.
2. Attend prewedding parties. Visit with out-of-town guests.
3. Confirm number of wedding guests to caterer.
4. Confirm staff assignments with minister.

One Week Before Wedding

1. Make final check with florist, photographer, baker, and musicians.
2. Remind all participants regarding rehearsal time and wedding time.
3. Check on any final alterations of clothing—bride's and groom's.
4. Pack for honeymoon trip.
5. Have newspaper release delivered.
6. Plan for someone to mail announcements on wedding day.
7. Pay the church obligations, including staff participants.

Two Days Before Wedding

1. Spend a quiet evening with your family.
2. Service car to be used for honeymoon.

One Day Before Wedding

1. Pack toiletries. Lay out clothes and going-away outfits.
2. Attend rehearsal and dinner; give gifts to attendants and to each other.

3. Give license to minister.
4. Go home early for a good night's rest.

On the Day of Wedding

1. Eat a substantial breakfast.
2. Groom makes out check to clergyman and gives it to best man to be delivered just before the ceremony procession.
3. Get dressed one and a half hours before wedding time. Bride and attendants should be completely dressed and ready for her informal pictures thirty minutes in advance of wedding time. Groom and best man should arrive twenty minutes in advance. Ushers should arrive one hour in advance.
4. After the reception, change into traveling outfit.
5. Thank everyone.
6. Leave for honeymoon.

After Wedding

1. Call home after arrival at honeymoon location.
2. Write postcards to family and friends while on honeymoon.
3. Have a wonderful time.
4. Remind parents to pay florist, caterer, musicians, and other obligations.

After Honeymoon

1. Unpack and get settled.
2. Exchange duplicate gifts.
3. Write thank-you notes.
4. Invite your first guests to dinner.
5. Call your minister and make an appointment for him to visit.

Floral Decorations

A wedding is a time for simplicity and good taste, with particular moderation advisable in the selection of floral displays.

There is no need for extreme decoration in the sanctuary; the use of arches, bells, trees, too many flowers, and candles are common abuses. One gets the impression at times that some families attempt to outdo others with ornament and display.

One well-known church allows the display of only one large bouquet for all weddings, however large or small. This rule prevents indulgence in competition and the desire to impress others.

Of course, the wish for a wedding of aesthetic beauty is normal, natural, and desirable. However, gaudiness and extremes should be avoided.

The basic principle is this: the simpler the decorations, the better. Decorations should neither distract from nor obscure the chancel furniture, the symbolism of the sanctuary, or the wedding service. The sanctuary itself should reflect in symbols and beauty the love of God and the spirit of Christ.

Flowers are needed for: bride, maid or matron of honor, bridesmaids, groom, best man, ushers (groomsmen), both mothers, grandmothers, both fathers, musicians, minister, bride's going-away corsage, chancel area, reception table, and perhaps the wedding cake.

Flowers of the Month

January	Carnation
February	Violet
March	Jonquil
April	Sweet pea
May	Lily of the valley
June	Rose
July	Larkspur
August	Gladiolus
September	Aster
October	Calendula
November	Chrysanthemum
December	Narcissus

Use of Flowers in the Church

The minister should inform local florists of the rules of his church with regard to wedding decorations, plus his own personal preferences regarding the same. Implicit understanding is needed with florists regarding the moving of chancel furniture, the places where flowers are to be located, and the use of tape and tacks.

When choosing floral arrangements, focus should be on the chancel and altar areas. Flowers usually are not allowed on the communion table or altar. A dark interior needs light shades of flowers; a large sanctuary with high ceilings needs tall arrangements.

If a small wedding is held in a large sanctuary, a few baskets of greenery or potted plants can define the perimeter of a smaller section to be used.

With formal weddings, flowers or ribbons are draped on the pews, to indicate the reserved seats for family members.

Some wedding florists use only greens with a series of candelabra. Be sure dripless candles are used or that a plastic sheet is placed beneath each candelabra.

Increasingly couples are using a memory-candle ritual as a part of the ceremony. A very large white decorative candle is placed behind the prie-dieu, on a stand or preferably on the communion table or altar. Two smaller tapered candles are on each side and are lighted when other chancel candles are lit. At the conclusion of the ceremony the bride and groom each take a lighted taper, together light the memory candle and extinguish the two tapers, symbolic of two lives blended into one. The florist should provide these, if they are wanted.

Since the sanctuary itself is rich in symbolism, it is quite unnecessary to try to fill the area with massive floral arrangements. It is far better to decorate the reception area with flowers and the table with a beautiful centerpiece.

Determination should be made of what to do with the sanctuary flowers after the weddings. Many choose to leave them for the Sunday-morning worship; then they may be distributed to the homebound and sick friends.

The Photographer

Wedding pictures are important to record the event, yet the wedding is not just for pictures. A photographer can be a joy, or he can be overbearing, demanding, and a nuisance. He can destroy the solemnity of the occasion.

Some shopping needs to be done in selecting an experienced, professional wedding photographer. In the photographer's interview, he should clearly indicate, in writing, the price, the number of proofs to be made, the size and number of prints, and the cost of additional prints. You should have a list of the pictures you want and suggested candid shots.

Most churches have restrictions regarding photographs taken during the wedding ceremony. Ushers should ask wedding guests arriving with cameras to please refrain from taking flash pictures in the sanctuary. It greatly distracts from the wedding ceremony to have camera noise, photographer movement, and flashing during the ceremony.

It is imperative that the photographer abides by the church's policies and does not take an inordinate amount of time in taking the posed shots. To leave guests standing in the reception room while the photographer dominates the wedding party is rude. No more than fifteen to twenty minutes should be allowed for this.

Possible Pictures

A few informal shots: in the dressing room or parlor of the bride, the bride with father, bride and maid of honor, bride with bridesmaids. (These should not be taken until all are dressed, about thirty minutes in advance of wedding time.)

In gathering place of groom, groom and minister, groom and best man, groom and attendants.

Picture of decorated chancel before guests arrive.

Picture of bride and father at the back of the aisle before processing to chancel.

Picture of bride and groom leaving the aisle during the recessional.

Pictures re-posed in sanctuary (either before or after the reception): bride and groom alone, with the bridesmaids, with the total wedding party, at the priedieu with minister, with each set of parents, with other members of the immediate family, with grandparents. Then a picture of the bride alone. In case of divorced parents, each one has the picture taken with the couple separately. Stepparents are included if relationships with the bride and groom are congenial.

Pictures taken at the reception: the table before the cake is cut, bride and groom cutting the cake and feeding each other, and other candid shots of special people (provide list of those wanted and someone to point them out).

The bride throwing her bouquet.

Pictures of the departure from the church and the getaway car for honeymoon.

Infants and Children

Some couples insist upon having children in the wedding party as flower girls or ring bearers. Such a decision is wrought with much risk. The children are not old enough to comprehend the meaning of the service. They are expected to behave as adults, when they are immature and have limited interest spans. Many embarrassing and unfortunate incidents have occurred, which were totally disruptive of the solemnity of a wedding. When great sums of money are being expended and months of preparation made for these high moments, it is unwise to wish children's participation, however cute they may be.

Some people bring infants and children to the church wedding, wanting them to have a memorable experience. Often infants are uncontrollable and unpredictable and may disrupt the most tender moments of a ceremony. Such selfish thoughtlessness destroys the ceremony for the couple and all the congregation.

The bride should arrange a nursery care with the church for infants and small children if persons with children are invited.

Transportation

Transportation arrangements should be made to the wedding place and reception for the wedding party, relatives, and special out-of-town guests. Usually three or four cars are necessary.

The Church's Wedding Policy

Each congregation should have a carefully prepared, official policy regarding wedding arrangements. This is essential for directing the ministerial staff, the business and custodial personnel, and the bridal family. There are, of course, scores of churches that have been the scenes of many weddings for years upon years, with no definite policies. Arrangements have been at the discretion of the pastor, policies changing with succeeding pastors. Other churches have had unwritten policies known generally by the membership. Some have adopted new plans for each individual marriage.

However, in order to avoid misunderstandings and to make the planning parties aware of the responsibilities involved, it seems best to have a definite policy.

This may already be determined by the specific denomination. In most cases, the local, legislative, policy-making body (such as the trustees, general board, or session) initiates such directives. For most effective use, the policy should be printed and made available to the bride at the initial conference about the wedding. Publication of the policy in the church newspaper is important, to inform the congregation.

The policy should cover such matters as: the church facilities available and the cost for members and nonmembers, the services the church staff renders, and reception possibilities, acceptable music, the number of premarital conferences expected, and rules regarding decorations, photographs, the use of rice and confetti, smoking, and consumption of alcoholic beverages.

The basic purpose of such a policy should not be to discourage church weddings. To the contrary, the church wishes to encourage its people to have sacred wedding services in the church. Hence, the policy should be sufficiently flexible to allow variations of taste and sufficiently modest so that none are discouraged financially. Usually, it is wise to give the pastor the authority to alter financial obligations if and when there is sufficient need, in his judgment.

Sample Church Policy

Presented here is a sample policy that one church has adopted. It may not be appropriate to follow where there is a large, multiple staff, and costs may vary for different churches.

Central Christian Church wants to render the best possible service to its members and friends. You are welcome to the use of our facilities.

The wedding ceremony is one of the most sacred rites of the church. It is the desire of the pastor and the church family to make every such ceremony a beautiful and worshipful experience. We extend to each wedding party every possible courtesy and assistance.

To make available our services, the following procedures have been adopted.

Minister

The minister shall officiate at all marriages in the church, except in unusual situations where other arrangements are made with the pastor. In the absence of the minister, another ordained staff member will be assigned.

Ministers of other denominations shall be free to use the facilities and perform the ceremony according to the rites of their respective church, subject to the approval of the pastor of this church.

The bride and groom shall arrange a premarital conference with the minister as far in advance of the ceremony as possible. This conference should be held before the announcements are made or invitations printed. The minister will provide literature and advice which will be helpful for properly preparing for marriage.

The pastor will conduct the rehearsal with the assistance of the cateress, if desired, on the evening before the wedding.

No specific charge is made for the minister's services except as in keeping with the usual custom. Such arrangement is private and not the church's responsibility.

Music

Music used with the ceremony should be in keeping with the sacredness and dignity of the wedding service.

When the organ is desired, the church organist is to be used unless another request is made through the minister who will also recommend a soloist if requested. Fees for the soloist and organist are a private arrangement and should be so arranged in advance.

Photographs

Photographs may not be taken during the ceremony proper. Pictures may be taken during the processional and recessional. After the recessional, the wedding party may return for as many pictures as are desired.

Floral Decorations

Florists are required to clear arrangements with the church receptionist prior to decorating the church, or any portion thereof.

Flowers used must be in clean, rust-free, leak-proof containers.

Only dripless candles may be used to prevent drippings on the floor; a protective covering under the candelabra is required. In the event of dripping on furniture, floor, or carpets, the florist shall be responsible for cleaning and reimbursement for damage.

Church premises shall be left as clean as possible after removal of decorations.

Rice and Confetti

Rice and confetti throwing is to be done outside the building, not on the inside.

Receptions

Receptions held in church building must be under the direction of staff cateress, unless other arrangements are made with the pastor.

The church's punch bowl, silver service, cups, silverware, and linens are available, if desired.

Use of Alcoholic Beverages

It is expected that members of the wedding party will refrain from alcoholic beverages immediately preceding both the rehearsal and the wedding. No alcoholic beverages are to be used in the punch. There shall be no smoking in the sanctuary, or reception room. The bride and groom shall make these rules known to all members of the wedding party.

Fees

FOR CEREMONY:

[Here the church's policy should include the areas where a wedding may be held, seating capacity of each, which areas are air-conditioned, the fee for each for both members and nonmembers, and the deposit required with reservation.]

FOR RECEPTION:

[Here are listed the areas where a reception may be held, the seating capacity of each, the table accessories, the services of the cateress, custodian, the fees involved, and the deposit required with reservation.]

Fees shall be paid to receptionist or financial secretary when reservations are made or in advance of wedding. Exceptions to these fees may be made by the minister where in his opinion the payment would be a hardship and might deprive the couple of a church wedding.

In case there is a need to request arrangements differing from those outlined, such requests should be made to the minister before the rehearsal and/or wedding. The cateress and custodian do not have authority to make changes from these policies.[2]

Clergyman's Fee

Today's salary schedules for ministers in most denominations make it unnecessary for the clergyman to depend upon wedding fees for his expenses. Ideally, he should perform all of his ministerial duties as a part of his vocation and be paid an adequate salary by the congregation, without dependence upon gratuities. Freedom from such dependence helps the minister to refuse the temptation to marry eloping lovers and those whom, in good conscience, he prefers not to marry.

However, it is a tradition that the minister be given a modest monetary gift as an expression of appreciation. This is a legitimate practice, and such a gift can be accepted without apology because the conscientious minister spends many hours in the preparation for and performing of a wedding. Because of the service rendered in a wedding ceremony and the amount of time consumed, if anyone deserves a gratuity, it is undoubtedly the minister.

Details-of-Wedding Form[3]

Wedding of:

_____

_____

1. Date of ceremony _____ Time_____
   Formal _____ Semiformal_____ Informal _____
2. Place ceremony will be held _____
   Estimate of attendance _____
3. Date of wedding rehearsal _____ Time_____
4. Will all be present for rehearsal? _____
   Will there be a rehearsal dinner? _____
5. Single ring _____ Double ring_____
   Will bride be given away? _____
6. Will there be music? _____ Organist? _____ Soloist? _____
7. Will there be a reception? _____
8. Plans for decorations _____
9. Plans for photographs (check church regulations)_____
   _____
10. Bride's attendants:
    Maid (or matron) of honor _____
    Bridesmaids _____
    Flower girl and/or ring-bearer _____
11. Groom's attendants:
    Best man _____
    Groomsmen _____
    Ushers _____

Schedule of interviews with clergyman or counselor:
            Date   Time

1. _____   _____
2. _____   _____
3. _____   _____
Date of interview with staff member in charge of arrangements
for church and reception rooms _____

Chapter Six

Wedding Costs

The success of a wedding does not depend on its expensiveness; what counts most is the spirit, sincerity, tasteful thoughtfulness, content, and preorganization that creates an atmosphere of joy and reverence. This need not be elaborate.

Every couple should determine their desires as to the type of wedding wanted and the expenses limitations they wish to impose.

True, weddings are much more expensive than when the bride's parents married. Wedding expenses used to be quite modest, clearly defined, and everyone knew who was responsible for what. The bride's parents hosted the wedding and paid all the bills. The groom and his parents paid for the minister, the rehearsal dinner, and the honeymoon. Today families are more flexible. Many times parents may state the amount they can afford. Expenses beyond that are paid by the bride, the groom, or his parents. In today's unpredictable economy, it is difficult to estimate expenses, except in most general terms. Edith Gilbert, a wedding consultant and author, estimates in terms of percentage of total costs (on basis of one hundred guests): 5 percent announcements and mailing; 10 percent photography; 25 percent clothing and gifts; 10 percent ceremony expenses; 40 percent reception, flowers, and music; 10 percent miscellaneous.[1]

In 1983 she estimated that a simple informal wedding was usually less than $2,000; a semiformal wedding averaged less than $5,000; and the large formal wedding costs to be unlimited, depending upon many factors.

There are ways to cut expenses, keeping simplicity in mind. Some of the most beautiful and uplifting have been the most modest and intimate.

A wedding and reception can be held at the church more reasonably than most other places, with the exception of the home. Most congregations charge only service costs—that is, what the staff workers require for their services, such as custodian, organist, and caterer. Nonmembers are charged a modest amount to cover utilities for the wedding ceremony location and another for the reception, to cover utilities, laundry, and breakage. Most churches forbid alcoholic beverages and discourage a full-scale dinner, which cuts the large percentage of wedding costs. The minister is usually offered the privilege of lowering the costs under certain circumstances of need, with the staff taking a proportionate cut.

Financial Obligations

Of the Bride

Engraving of invitations and announcements
Mailing of invitations, cards, and announcements
Transportation for attendants to and from church
Hotel bills for her attendants, when her parents cannot accommodate them
Organist
Soloist
Rental of church and custodial fees
Wedding reception
Groom's ring
Bride's trousseau
Wedding photographs and video tapes
Gifts to the bridesmaids and maid (or matron) of honor
Bridesmaids' flowers
Church decorations
Gift to groom
Bride's wedding dress and accessories
Floral decorations for ceremony and reception
Music for church and reception
Bride's doctor's visit and blood test

Of the Groom

Bride's engagement and wedding rings
Marriage license
Bachelor dinner (optional)
Rehearsal dinner
Gift to bride
Groom's wedding attire
Groom's doctor's visit and blood test
Bride's flowers
Transportation for male attendants to and from church
Clergyman's fee
Corsages for the mothers of the bride and the groom
Boutonnieres for best man, ushers, groomsmen, groom's
    father, and the minister
Gifts to male attendants and ushers
Ties and gloves for attendants (optional)
Hotel bill for his attendants from out of town
Bride's going-away corsage
Honeymoon expenses

Bridesmaid's Expenses

Purchase of bridesmaid's dress and all accessories
An individual gift to the couple
Sharing in a shower or luncheon for the bride
Transportation to and from location of wedding

Ushers' (Groomsmens') Expenses

Rental of wedding attire
Transportation to and from location of wedding
An individual gift to the couple
A bachelor dinner may be given by the ushers (grooms-
    men), the best man, or the groom's father

Guest Expenses

The groom's parents pay their own transportation and
    lodging expenses, as do out-of-town guests. The par-

ents of the bride and groom may help in securing accommodations at the home of friends for bridesmaids and groomsmen.

One gradual change is occurring: the groom and his family are taking a more active role in planning of, preparing for, and sharing in the expenses of the wedding. Emily Post indicates that it is no longer considered an insult to the bride and her family if the groom makes the offer. The bride's family should never initiate the request.

The Budget

A carefully prepared, realistic wedding budget will help make preparations smoother. The marriage will get off to a good start if responsible judgment is exercised.

Some of the items that should be investigated and estimated at the beginning are included in a suggested form by Emily Post.

Budgets[2]

	For a Large Formal Wedding		For a Simple Wedding at Home	
	Type	Amount	Type	Amount
Invitations	Engraved or thermographed	$_____	Handwritten notes or telephone calls	$10
Food	Sit-down dinner	$_____	Sandwiches, snacks	$100
Beverages	Champagne, liquor	$_____	Punch (with or without liquor)	$25–$50
Flowers	Church, reception, attendants	$_____	Fresh from garden or 2 vases for "altar"	$0 $30
Cake	3-tiered from bakery	$_____	Baked by Aunt Doris	$0
Photographs	Formal and candid (commercial)	$_____	Taken by Uncle John	$0
Caterer	Professional	$_____	Friends and relatives	$0
Hall rental	(where applicable)	$_____	None	
Music	Orchestra	$_____	Tapes or records (rented)	$20
Wedding dress	From bridal salon	$_____	Borrowed from best friend or favorite "old" dress	
Clergy fee	Substantial	$_____	Small donation or gift if ceremony performed by friend	
Sexton's fee		$_____	None	$0
Limousines	For bridal party	$_____	None	$0

Chapter Seven

Duties and Responsibilities of Wedding-Party Participants[1]

Duties of the Bride and Her Family

Bride

Determines the type of wedding wanted.

Selects her attendants and notifies them of the dates and place of the rehearsal and wedding.

Selects the style and color of the bridesmaids' dresses; however she usually does not pay for them.

Purchases the wedding ring for her future husband.

Chooses the photographer for the wedding.

Chooses her glassware and dinnerware patterns.

Provides a gift for each of her attendants.

Acknowledges receipt of each wedding gift with a personal note.

Buys her future husband a wedding gift.

Bride's Family

Pays for decorations and flowers for the church and reception.

If the bride's family is wealthy, it may pay for the bridal attendants' dresses. The bride's family furnishes the headdresses and bouquets for bridal attendants.

Bride and Her Mother

Set the date, place, and time of the ceremony.

Schedule the church, pastor, organist and soloist.

Select the invitations and make up the guest list (after conferring with the groom and his mother) for wedding and reception guests. They address and mail the invitations.

Duties of the Groom

Purchases the bride's engagement and wedding rings.

Selects his attendants and notifies them of the dates and place of the rehearsal and wedding.

Arranges for the rehearsal dinner.

Gives the bride lists of relatives and friends whom he wishes invited to the wedding and reception.

Buys a gift for each of his attendants.

Buys his bride a wedding gift.

Provides ties and boutonnieres for his attendants, as regional customs demand.

Plans the honeymoon trip and makes necessary arrangements.

Purchases the bride's bouquet and the mother's corsages.

Purchases the wedding license.

Responsibilities of Attendants

All Bridal Attendants

Buy their own dresses or suits and accessories, except as otherwise listed.

Must attend the wedding rehearsal on time.

Keep all appointments related to clothes fitting and prewedding parties.

Send a wedding gift to the bride and groom, either as individuals or as a group.

Are invited to all parties given for the bride. Parties given for both bride and groom include invitations to both bride and groom attendants. The groom's attendants are invited to all stag parties.

Maid (or Matron) of Honor

The maid of honor is the bride's dearest unmarried friend or relative. The matron of honor is the bride's dearest married friend or relative. Often she is the bride's sister. She:

> May help the bride to compile the guest list, to address the invitations, and assist in many ways.
> Attends the rehearsal.
> Arranges the bride's train as the procession forms in the rear of the church and again at the altar if necessary and straightens it behind the bride as she turns for the recessional.
> Holds the bride's bouquet during the ring exchange.
> Carries the groom's ring during the ceremony (unless there is a ring bearer) and gives it to the minister at the appropriate time.
> Signs the wedding certificate.
> If the bride wears a veil, she helps lift it back on her head at the end of the ceremony.
> In the recessional, if the attendants leave in couples, she walks with the best man.
> Stands in the receiving line, next to the groom.
> Assists the bride in changing clothes and packing for her trip.
> Sees that no tricks in bad taste are played.
> If both a maid and a matron of honor are used, the bride must decide which one will stand by her during the ceremony. The one chosen will process directly in front of the bride and her father (unless there is a flower girl and/or a ring bearer).

The Best Man

The best man is the groom's primary attendant. He may be the groom's brother, father, cousin, or a friend. He:

> Gives a wedding gift to the couple.
> Usually entertains the bridal couple, or he may give the bachelor party if no other arrangements have been made.

Sometimes sends flowers to the hotel where the bride and groom spend their first night.

Wears the same attire as the groom, but his boutonniere is different.

Helps the bride's mother with last-minute errands.

Aids the groom in every way possible in preparation for the wedding.

Protects the groom from pranks and does not participate in practical jokes played on the bride and groom.

Attends the rehearsal and assists in seeing that male attendants are on time.

Helps the groom dress for the wedding and drives him to the church at least a half hour before wedding time.

Waits with groom until the processional.

Signs the wedding certificate.

He delivers the license to the minister for his signature.

Gives the clergyman his fee, inconspicuously, in a plain, sealed envelope.

Accompanies the groom to the altar, carrying the bride's ring until the time the minister asks for it in the ceremony. If the groom wears gloves, the best man holds them.

Usually he does not stand in the receiving line unless he is the father and the bride chooses to have the fathers in it.

If the reception is at a place other than the church, he chauffeurs the couple and maid of honor to the place of the reception; he may also take some of the bridesmaids.

Proposes the first toast to the couple at the reception and reads any congratulatory messages.

If no one else is assigned, he is responsible for seeing that the guest book is in place for signing.

Makes arrangements for the "getaway car." He assists the groom in redressing, packing, and placing the luggage in the car, and sees them off if they leave by plane.

Takes the groom's wedding clothes from the reception area to the groom's home and to the rental place the next day.

Bridesmaids

The bride decides how many bridesmaids she wants, ranging from one to six.

Bridesmaids are the bride's unmarried or married sisters, relatives, or friends. If the groom has a sister of suitable age, it is customary to have her as a bridesmaid when the wedding party is large. They:

> Attend the rehearsal and rehearsal dinner, seated alternately with the ushers.
> Walk alone or in pairs and sometimes with an usher in the processional, depending upon the wishes of the minister and bride.
> In the recessional bridesmaids are usually escorted by an usher or with another bridesmaid, depending upon the custom of the church or minister.
> Stand in the receiving line at the reception, greeting the guests, or they may mingle with the guests, depending upon the bride's decision.

Ushers (Groomsmen)

The number of ushers varies with the wedding. One usher for each fifty expected guests. There should be an equal number of ushers in the chancel wedding party as there are bridal attendants. All ushers:

> Wear similar attire.
> Attend the wedding rehearsal where they will be given detailed instructions.
> Send the bridal couple a wedding gift as individuals or as a group.
> Are invited to all parties given for the couple, unless it is a family party.
> Arrive at the church one hour before the processional starts.
> Line up at the left of front door in the vestibule of the church, enabling them to offer the right arm to each lady guest.
> Mingle with the guests at the reception.

Head Usher

Is a close mature friend of groom.

Is responsible for seeing that ushers arrive at church on time for rehearsal and wedding.

Takes notes of rehearsal instructions and special assignments.

Arrives one hour in advance of announced processional time. He synchronizes the watches of organist and minister with his own.

Takes the groom's and best man's boutonnieres to the dressing room and helps pin boutonnieres on other ushers.

Has special instructions noted regarding reserved sections and seating of guests and informs the ushers of the seating plan.

He watches the seating to see that guests are seated uniformly on both sides.

Gives the signal at the proper time for appointed ushers to light candles, seat grandparents, seat groom's mother, seat bride's mother, draw the aisle ribbons, pull back the aisle canvas, close the doors after the processional, open door for recessional, return for the bride's mother, return for the groom's mother, untie the aisle ribbons.

Junior Bridesmaids

Junior bridesmaids usually are sisters or relatives of the bride or the groom who are between the ages of twelve and fourteen. Their duties compliment those of the bridesmaids.

Flower Girl

The flower girl is a small child related either to the bride or to the groom or is the child of a best friend. In the processional she is placed in front of the bride and her father.

As she walks, she may strew petals in the aisle, from a small basket of flowers that she carries.

Wears a party dress or a replica of the bridesmaids'

dresses, for which her parents are responsible, plus a garland of flowers in her hair, which the bride furnishes.

Attends the rehearsal.

Is not invited to the bridal parties, but her mother is, and her parents are invited to parties for the couples.

May or may not be a part of the recessional and does not stand in the receiving line.

Ring Bearer

The ring bearer is a small boy, usually a relative of the bride or groom or the child of a close friend.

He carries a small, white satin pillow on which the wedding rings are attached with a light silk stitch. Often the real rings are not used on the pillow.

In the procession he precedes the flower girl, if there is one; if there is no flower girl, he precedes the bride and her father.

May leave the wedding party and sit with his mother after the best man unfastens the rings from the pillow, or if the real rings are not used, he may leave when the wedding party reaches the altar.

Usually takes no part in the recessional or in the receiving line.

Chapter Eight

Wedding Music

Because music is usually an integral part of the marriage service, the minister cannot be indifferent to the type of music used, nor can he totally abdicate making decisions regarding it to the whim or fancy of the bride.

The choice of music can amplify the important trend away from popular, secular, love songs, toward more sacred, God-centered music; from songs expressing human love of bride and groom, to music that is dignified and reverent.

The bride may be totally unaware of what is fitting music for a religious service or too inexperienced musically to have good judgment regarding appropriate selections. Too much music is chosen on the basis of its being the romantic, secular selections that were the couple's favorites during their courtship. Other couples choose popular show music they consider entertaining. The minister might suggest that these selections be sung at the rehearsal dinner or the bridal shower or party or at the reception following the wedding, if the bride is insistent that they be used.

Selecting Music

The minister has a responsibility to give early directives for the selection of music that will help maintain the dignity, meaning, and spiritual basis of the marriage service. Wedding music should be God centered. Each minister should tactfully direct this area according to his church's policy, without injuring the feelings of the persons involved. The minister may submit a listing of what his church considers appropriate or

101

acceptable music, from which the bride and groom may choose. Some ministers are rigidly strict; others prefer to indicate the ideal music but retain some flexibility. I have always believed it better to sacrifice quality occasionally if rigidity jeopardizes a good relationship with those who have predetermined selections and have no disposition to change them.

The much used traditional Wagner and Mendelssohn wedding marches are being omitted from marriage services in many churches and replaced by great processional hymns. The reasons have much merit. The "Here Comes the Bride" chorus from Wagner's *Lohengrin* was never intended for church use. In the opera, this excerpt occurs when the bride and groom enter the bridal chamber and the bed is being readied. The music is even more incongruous for use at a wedding when one considers that, before the act is over, the bridegroom has murdered a rival and is forced to abandon his wife forever. The Mendelssohn music was composed as an accompaniment to Shakespeare's *A Midsummer Night's Dream.* A musical fantasy, attention is centered on a workman named Bottom, who is transformed into a donkey. The donkey courts and bewitches a fairy. The play is filled with sensuality and magic and is inappropriate for a Christian wedding.[1]

It takes a diplomatic, courageous, and persuasive minister to break with the popular practices that have infiltrated the church and to win the cooperation of his church leadership, membership, and of the wedding parties in particular. If possible, however, he should begin somehow, somewhere, to raise the standards and choose music that is consistent with the church's worship.

Some ministers prefer only organ music for the wedding. The organist who plays at the wedding should be the regular church organist or assistant organist, since they are familiar with the church's instrument and their ability is known and accepted by the minister. If the bride desires a friend to play the organ, approval should be obtained from the music committee, the minister, or the church organist.

When vocal music is desired, it may be supplied by the choir, an ensemble, or a soloist. When it is desired that there be a vocal soloist, it is wise for the minister to recommend a singer from among the church singers, rather than to have a friend of the bride sing, who may or may not have the ability or the proper repertoire to make the spiritual contribution. If the bride desires a particular person to sing, it might be suggested that the singer audition with the organist for approval a month prior to the wedding.

Wedding Bells and Chimes

The organ chimes may be played at the end of the ceremony, just before the recessional. If not at that time, the chimes can be a part of the recessional music or postlude.

Church bells may be played at the conclusion of the ceremony.

Lists of Appropriate Music

Following are three listings of appropriate music for the Christian wedding.

Contemporary Wedding Music

BOOKS CONTAINING CONTEMPORARY WEDDING MUSIC

1. *Everything for the Wedding Soloist* (Carol Stream, Ill: Hope Pub., 1981).
2. *Folk Songs for Weddings* (Carol Stream, Ill.: Hope Pub., 1972).
3. *Music for the Christian Wedding*, Floyd W. Hawkins, ed. (Kansas City, Mo.: Lillenas, 1968).
4. *Our Sacred Day*, John Wilson, comp. (Carol Stream, Ill.: Hope Pub., 1968).
5. *The Bond of Love* (Kansas City, Mo.: Lillenas, 1979).

Songs listed below are numbered to indicate which book they may be found in.

PREPROCESSIONAL VOCAL MUSIC

Solos by Subject

Thankfulness
God Is Here (Blackley) 5
For These Gifts (Wilson) 1
Sometimes (Henry Mancini) 1

Commitment

Ode to Joy (Sutherlin) 2
Entreat Me Not to Leave Thee (Oosting) 2
Entreat Me Not to Leave Thee (Gounod, arr. by Jack Schrader) 1
I Will Follow (Avery and Marsh) 1
Song of Ruth (Gary Hallquist) 1
Whither Thou Goest (Paul Liljestrand) 1

Family

Happy the Home When God Is There (John Wilson) 4
Thank You for These Gifts (John Wilson) 1

Prayer

Our Prayer (Riley) 5
A Wedding Prayer (E. Margaret Clarkson) 4
God Bless This Marriage (Hanks) 2
The Lord's Prayer (Isenlee) 1

Love

Wedding Song (There Is Love), (Paul Stookey) 2, 1
The Joy of Living (March) 5
Love Is (Fettke) 5
When You Created Love (Fettke) 5
O Perfect Love (White) 2
The Love That Lasts a Lifetime (Bryan Leech) 1
The Gift of Love (Hopson) 2
O Perfect Love (Harry Burleigh) 4
So Love I Thee (Grieg) 2

Trust

Psalm 128 (Dailey) 5

FOLK SONGS

You Made Us for Each Other (Innes) 2
The Two Shall Be as One (Wilson) 2

CONTEMPORARY PROCESSIONAL MUSIC

Trumpet Tune (Jeremiah Clarke, arr. by John Wilson) 4
Bridal Chorus (Richard Wagner, arr. by Martin West) 4

SOLOS FOLLOWING RING EXCHANGES AND VOWS

    Join Us Now (Dyer) 5
    With This Ring (Roger Copeland) 1

HOLY COMMUNION SONGS

    The Bond of Love (Skillings) 5
    When You Created Love (Frettke) 5
    Let Us Break Bread Together (John Wilson) 2

UNITY-CANDLE SONGS

    And Now We Join (Sten Halfvarson) 1
    O God of Love (Janet Niceum) 3
    Join Us Now (Dyer) 5
    When Two Become One (Dyer) 5
    May the God of Love (John Wilson) 2
    The Bond of Love (Skillings) 5

BENEDICTION SONGS

    Wedding Benediction (Martin West) 4
    May the God of Love (John Wilson) 2
    Psalm 128 (Dailey) 5
    May the Grace of Christ Our Savior (Henry Gaunt-
       lett) 4
    May the Grace of Christ (George Stebbins) 3
    Corporate Prayer (Floyd) 2
    Wedding Benediction (John Wilson) 1
    Bridal Prayer (Roger Copeland) 1

LOVE SONGS FOR RECEPTION, PARTIES, WEDDING DINNER

    One Hand, One Heart (Sondheim and Bernstein) 1
    Christian Love Song (Marsha Stevens) 1
    When God Gave Me You (Lillenas) 3
    Sunrise, Sunset (from *Fiddler on the Roof*)
    Endless Love (Lionel Richie)
    Longer (Daniel Fogelberg)

Feelings (Morris Albert)
Twelfth Day of Never (Paul Francis Webster and Jerry
  Livingston)

Traditional Wedding Music

PREPROCESSIONAL ORGAN MUSIC

All Creatures of Our God and King (Geistliche Kirchen-
  gesäng)
Great Is Thy Faithfulness (William M. Runyan)
Jesus, Thou Joy of Loving Hearts (Quebec)
Praise, My Soul, the King of Heaven (Goss)

PREPROCESSIONAL VOCAL MUSIC (SOLO OR CHOIR)

Entreat Me Not to Leave Thee (Gorton)
God So Loved the World (Stainer)
Love Is Kind and Suffers Long (Capetown)
O God Our Help in Ages Past (Croft)
O Lord Most Holy (Franck)
Thanks Be to Thee (Handel)
The King of Love My Shepherd Is

PROCESSIONAL MUSIC

Love Divine, All Loves Excelling (John Zundell)
Now Thank We All Our God (Johann Crüger)
Praise Ye the Lord, the Almighty (Lobe den Herren)
Thine Is the Glory (Handel)
Trumpet Air (Purcell)
Wedding March (Mendelssohn)

WITHIN THE CEREMONY

A Wedding Prayer (Diggle)
The Pledge (Black)
O Perfect Love (Barnby)
Take Our Lives (Cesar Malon)
The Lord's Prayer (Malotte)

RECESSIONAL

> Joyful, Joyful We Adore Thee (Beethoven)
> Guide Me, O Thou Great Jehovah (Hughes)
> Savior, Like a Shepherd Lead Us (Bradbury)
> How Firm a Foundation (Early American Melody)
> Psalm 19—The Heavens Declare Thy Glory (Marcello)

LOVE SONGS FOR RECEPTION, PARTIES, SHOWERS, OR WEDDING DINNERS

> I Love You Truly (Carrie Jacobs Bond)
> Because (Guy D'Hardelot)
> From This Day Forth
> O Promise Me (Reginald de Koven)
> So I Love Thee
> When God Gave Me You
> I Love Thee (*Ich Liebe Dich*) (Edvard Grieg)

Classical Wedding Music

PRELUDES

> *Bach*
> My Spirit, Be Joyful!
> Our Father Which Art in Heaven
> My Heart Ever Faithful (ed. by Gigout)
> Jesu, Joy of Man's Desiring
> Sheep May Safely Graze
> Deck Thyself, My Soul, With Gladness
> Sleepers, Wake!
> In Thee Is Gladness
> Rejoice, Beloved Christians
> If Thou Art Near
> St. Ann Fugue
> Allegro (Concerto in A Minor, after Vivaldi)
> Air in D (also other Airs and Adagios)
> Siciliano in C Minor
> Sinfonia to Cantata 142
> From Heaven Above (two settings)
> Now Thank We All Our God (ed. by Fox)

In Dulci Jubilo
Air for G String
Little G Minor, Cathedral
Lord Jesus Christ Be Present Now
Loving Jesus, We Are Here

Bairstow
Evening Song

Batiste
Offertoire

Bennett
God Is a Spirit

Beethoven
Adagio
Andante Cantabile From Symphony V
Moonlight Sonata

Boellmann
Gothic Suite (Chorale and Prayer)

Brahms
A Lovely Rose Is Blooming
My Faithful Heart Rejoices

Buxtehude
Fugue in C

Corelli
Adagio in B Minor

Couperin
Benedictus

Diggle
Salut D'Amour

Dubois
Wedding Mass, Selections

Franck
Cantabile in A Minor, B Minor, and E Major
Adagio (Fantasie in C)
Prelude, Fugue and Variation

Frescobaldi
Toccata per l'Elevazione

Guilmant
Movements From Sonatas

Handel
Water Music (Allegro, Air, Allegro Maestoso)
Royal Fireworks Music (Overture, The Rejoicing, The
    Peace, Finale, Largo)
The Faithful Shepherd
Pastorale Symphony (*Messiah*)

Hokanson
Crown With Thy Benediction

James
Meditation à Ste. Clothilde

Karg-Elert
O God, Thou Faithful God
Claire de Lune

Manz
"Hyfrydol" and other chorale improvisations

Marcello
Psalm 18, Psalm 20

Massenet
The Angelus

McKinley
Cantalene

Mendelssohn
Adagio (Sonata I)
Allegro Maestoso (Sonata II)
Hear My Prayer
Movements From Sonatas

Peters
Aria, Op. 51

Purcell
Trumpet Tune and Air
Trumpet Voluntary

Purvis
Canzona on "Leibster Jesu"
Pastorale on "Forest Green"
Communion

Rheinberger
Sonatas

Smart
An Evening Prayer

Vaughan Williams
Prelude on "Rhosymedre"

Weaver
Bell Benedictus (Harp and Chimes)

Wely
Andante in F

Wetzler
Processional on "Westminster Abbey"

Widor
Andante Cantabile (Organ Symphony IV)

Wright
Brother James' Air

VOCAL SOLOS

Bach
My Heart Ever Faithful
Jesus, Joy of Man's Desiring
God My Shepherd Walks Beside Me

Bach-Bunnes
O Love That Casts Out Fear

Bach-Diak
Trust in the Lord

Barnby
O Perfect Love

Beethoven
I Love Thee

Bitgood
Though I Speak With the Tongue of Men and of Angels

Black
The Pledge

Brahms
Lord, Lead Us Still

Bunjes
Love Divine

Buxtehude
My Jesus Is My Lasting Joy
Lord, Who at Cana's Wedding Feast
O Father, All Creating

Burleigh
O Perfect Love

Clokey
Set Me as a Seal

Davies
The Lord's My Shepherd

Diggle
A Wedding Prayer

Dvořak
God Is My Shepherd
I Will Sing New Songs of Gladness

Franck
O Lord Most Holy

Galbraith
Holy Spirit, Breath of Love

Gorton
Entreat Me Not

Gounod
Entreat Me Not to Leave Thee

Grieg
Ich Liebe Dich (I Love Thee)

Handel
Largo (Wedding Lyrics)
Thanks Be to Thee
Where Ere You Walk

Helder-Bunjes
The Lord My Shepherd Is

Hildack
Where'er Thou Goest

Jacob
Brother James' Air (Psalm 23)

Klecher-Wick
Bless Our Vows

Kittel
O Father, Son and Holy Ghost

LaForge
Father, Guide and Defend Us

Lippe
How Do I Love Thee

Lloyd
O Christ Who Once Has Deigned

Lovelace
We Lift Our Hearts to Thee

Malotte
The Lord's Prayer

Mendelssohn
The Voice That Breathed O'er Eden
If With All Your Heart

Mozart
Alleluja

Polack
The Lord Be With You

Root
Love Never Faileth

Rowley
A Wedding Prayer

Trew
Brother James' Air

Thiman
Thou Wilt Keep Him in Perfect Peace

Vaughan Williams
The Call

Willan
Eternal Love

Williams
A Wedding Prayer

Wood
God Made Thee Mine (by any of the following: Burleigh, Clokey, Clough-Leighter, Pedrette, Fox, Willan, Sowerby, Overby, or Barnby)
O Perfect Love

ANTHEMS FOR CHOIR OR ENSEMBLE

Bach
Now Thank We All Our God

Franck
O Lord Most Holy

Handel
Thanks Be to Thee
The King of Love My Shepherd Is

Stainer
God So Loved the World

PROCESSIONALS

Bach
Adagio in A Minor
Adagio (Toccata, Adagio, and Fugue in C)
Air (Orchestral Suite in D Major)

Allebreve in D
Arioso in A
Sheep May Safely Graze
Sinfonia (Wedding Cantata 196)

Beethoven
Hymn of Joy

Biggs
Bell Symphony

Bloch
Four Wedding Marches

Campra
Rigandoon

Clarke
Processional March

Clokey
Processional (A Wedding Suite)
Recessional (A Wedding Suite)

Coke-Jephcott
Bishop's Promenade

Costa
Triumphal March

Dubois
Psalm XVIII

Grieg
March Triumphant

Handel
A Trumpet Voluntary
Processional in G Minor
Solemn Processional

Haydn-Brahms
Chorale, "St. Antoni"

Kreckek
Nuptial Procession

Mendelssohn
Allegro Mestoso (Sonata 4)
Wedding March (Midsummer Night's Dream)

Purcell
Trumpet Tune
Trumpet Tune in D Major
Trumpet Voluntary in D

Purvis
Jubilate Deo

Stanley
Processional in G Major
Trumpet Tune

Vierne-Carillon
Twenty-four Pieces in Free Style
Finale (Symphonie 1)

Wagner
Wedding March (Lohengrin)

Wesley
Choral Song

Widor
Toccata (Fifth Symphony)
Nuptial March

RECESSIONAL

Dubois
Grand Choeur

Karg-Elert
Now Thank We All Our God

Marcello
The Heavens Declare

Tombelle
March Pontificale

Widor
Selected Movements Symphonies V & VI

FANFARES

> *Bax*
> For the Wedding of Elizabeth II
>
> *Purcell*
> Fanfare in C

Chapter Nine

The Wedding Rehearsal

The best assurance of a beautiful and orderly wedding service is a thorough rehearsal.

It is generally necessary to have a rehearsal for every wedding that has a processional planned. The exception is the informal, "stand-up" wedding where no guests or only the immediate families are present. In the latter case, the minister usually can give brief instructions to the persons involved just prior to the wedding service.

Time for Rehearsal

The most common and effective time for the rehearsal usually is the night before the wedding. To have it prior to this time risks all the participants not being present or those present forgetting some of the important details. To have the rehearsal on the day of the wedding is to overcrowd an already busy day for the bride and her party. When a wedding dinner is planned, it is most convenient to have the rehearsal prior to the dinner the night before the wedding; or the rehearsal may follow the dinner. One hour's time should be allowed for the rehearsal.

It is imperative that all participants be present and on time for the rehearsal, including the ushers, the parents of the bride and groom, and the musicians. It is the bride's responsibility to notify each person of the rehearsal time.

The Rehearsal Director

The minister is in charge of the rehearsal instructions, unless a wedding counselor is hired. He should be the "take-charge" person, knowing the exact details, being discreet, decisive, and thorough. Occasionally, the bride may want a florist, a wedding specialist, or her mother to conduct the rehearsal. Generally, such practices are discouraged because they can lead to confusion, unless there is prior clearing of details with the minister. It is a much better practice for the processional details to be discussed with the minister and decisions made during one of the prewedding conferences, so that the minister can direct the rehearsal with decisiveness. If there are alternate ideas projected during the rehearsal, it can be confusing to the participants. The minister should give attention to every detail, taking nothing for granted, so that every person knows what is expected of him and when. In some of the large congregations, where the demands upon the minister's time are many, a wedding hostess may be assigned to direct rehearsals for him. She, of course, would be trained in the details and procedures used by the minister.

The Wedding-Service Plan

A list of participants should be prepared by the bride and handed to the minister prior to the rehearsal.

When the participants have arrived for the rehearsal, the minister should invite all to the front of the sanctuary, and ask that they be seated. He then introduces himself and the organist, greets the members of the wedding party, and announces the wedding procedure.

The minister should announce the wedding-service plan and time at the outset of the rehearsal.

A generally accepted procedure is: prelude music (to begin fifteen minutes prior to announced time of wedding); seating of guests by ushers; candles lighted; groom's parents ushered to seats; bride's mother ushered to seat; aisle runner unrolled; vocal music; the wedding processional; the marriage ceremony; the wedding recessional; bride's parents ushered out; groom's parents ushered out; congregation dismissed.

Slight alterations can be made in this procedure in accord with local policy, practice, or desire.

Ushering Instructions

Much of the smooth orderliness of the wedding depends upon the ushers' finesse and alertness. Ushers should not be flippant or loud talking. They should be cordial with each guest, yet not use the occasion for visiting with the guests or joking with one another.

One usher should be selected as the head usher, who will be in charge.

Ushers should arrive one hour in advance of the wedding time to check the lights, see that the proper doors are opened, to help distribute flowers, if asked, and to seat early guests. Guests should be seated as they arrive, to eliminate lingering and visiting in the foyer and possible delay of processional.

In some areas of the country and with the more formal weddings, pew cards may be used. They are sent out to special and family guests with the designated honor section. Each guest, as he or she enters the church informs the usher that he or she is to sit in the reserved bride's or groom's section. Sometimes the ushers are furnished a list of the guests to be seated in reserved sections. The florist identifies the proper number of rows reserved by decorating with special ribbons.

If a guest fails to inform the usher on which side she is to sit, the usher may ask in a quiet voice, "Are you a family or friend of the bride or groom?" Relatives and honored friends of the bride are seated on the *left* side, in the front of the church. The front row or pew is for the bride's mother only, until she is joined by her husband.

Relatives and honored friends of the groom are seated on the *right* side, in the front of the church. The front row or pew is for the groom's parents only.

If after seating many guests, the arrangement seems unbalanced, the later arriving guests should be seated to help equalize both sides of the sanctuary. The usher might say to later arrivals, "Would you mind sitting on the _____ side? There are better seats there."

Lady With Male Escort

The usher offers his right arm to the lady guest. Her escort follows a few steps behind. If several couples arrive simultaneously or together and time is running out or there is a shortage of ushers, an usher may offer his right arm to the oldest lady and the other couples follow, ladies walking first. They sit together as couples.

Lady Without Male Escort

An usher escorts each lady unless there is a shortage of ushers and time; in that event he escorts the oldest lady and the others in the party follow a few steps behind. Each is seated in the same pew. Young ladies may be escorted by an usher, or they may follow their parents when they are seated.

Men Arriving Alone

Unless the man is aged or feeble, the usher does not offer his arm. He leads or walks beside the male guest, showing him to a seat.

Small Children

Small children are not escorted by an usher; rather they follow their mother when she is ushered to her seat.

Seating the Bride's and Groom's Mothers

When the announced hour of the wedding has arrived and all guests are seated, the groom's mother is escorted by the ushers to the first or second pew on the right side. Her husband follows behind them.

The mother of the bride is escorted by another usher to the first or second pew on the left side.

In the event the parents of either bride or groom are divorced, the bride's mother and stepfather are seated in the front pew on the left side; the bride's father sits in the next pew with his present wife. The same seating arrangements are followed for the groom's parents on the right side. Whatever the circumstances, if on speaking terms, the bride's father should present his daughter for marriage. For the couple's sake, all personal ill-feelings should be transcended, to make it a happy and special day.

If any guests arrive after the mother is seated, they are seated in the back pew.

Seating Charts

Church With Center Aisle

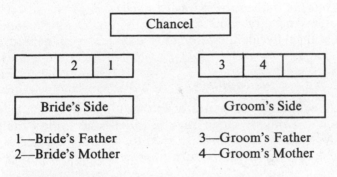

1—Bride's Father   3—Groom's Father
2—Bride's Mother   4—Groom's Mother

Church Without Center Aisle

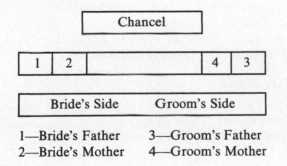

1—Bride's Father   3—Groom's Father
2—Bride's Mother   4—Groom's Mother

Aisle Ribbons and Aisle Canvas

In some areas, with the more formal wedding procession, aisle ribbons are used to enclose the section where guests are seated. The ribbons are folded and attached to the first aisle post beyond the reserved section. Two ushers come forward, take the ribbon, placing it over each aisle post the entire length of the aisle. Then they fasten the ribbon to the last pew post.

The aisle canvas or bridal carpet is seldom used anymore. If it is requested, the folded or rolled canvas is placed at the front of the chancel steps, with one end attached there. Just before the processional is to begin, two ushers go forward, each takes a corner of the canvas, and together they pull it the length of the aisle. The procession may then proceed.

Ushers and the Processional

Ushers may walk in pairs, leading the processional, or each one may escort a bridal attendant.

Ushers not in the processional and chancel participation will close the sanctuary doors following the processional, stand in front of them during the ceremony, and then open them for the recessional.

Ushering out the Mothers

Following the recessional of the wedding party, the ushers escort the mothers out in reverse order—the bride's mother first, with the father following, then the groom's mother. If requested, the ushers may return to escort the grandmothers as well.

The remainder of the guests may be signaled out by one or two ushers, one row at a time on each side, starting from the front and working back. Or the head usher may come to the front of the aisle, lift up his arms so guests stand and are dismissed by the usher's appropriate gesture.

Lighting of Candles

It is increasingly common for the candles to be lighted before the first guests arrive. If this is the preference, then two ushers usually do it, approximately thirty minutes before the announced time. When there is an unusually large number of candles, the florist may choose to do the lighting.

If candlelight is preferred as a part of the service, it may be done by ushers or by two other friends, either male or female, chosen by the bride and groom.

At the appropriate time, the candlelighters walk together from the rear of the sanctuary, carrying the lighters. In the event that one goes out, it can be lighted from the other. The candlelighters begin from the outside of the candelabra, lighting the candles one by one, in unison. When all are lighted, they meet at the center and extinguish the lighters. If they are ushers, they then proceed to the rear of the sanctuary; if not, they are seated in the front row, one to the far left and the other to the far right.

Processional Instructions

It is usually best to begin the rehearsal by giving instructions to those in the procession. The minister asks each one individually to come forward as he calls their position and places them where they will stand for the beginning of the ceremony. Care should be taken that the spacing is proper (*see* Diagrams of Arrangements) and that each person makes a mental note of his position in relationship to the chancel steps and others in the party. While all are in their places, the minister explains about the door from where each will come, the spacing, the kind of walk, and how they will stand while the bride and her father process.

As a general rule, the groom, best man, and minister enter the sanctuary from a side front door, following the wedding-march call. They walk slowly, erectly, and approximately four feet apart. The groomsmen may come from this location as well; from the rear of the sanctuary, by twos; or each groomsman may escort a bridesmaid. The bride should make the choice of which way this should be done prior to the rehearsal, so that there is no question. When the men reach their positions at the chancel steps, they face toward the center aisle, with hands either at the sides or folded in front, with left over right (this should be consistent with all the male attendants). The men should have pleasant smiles as they watch the bridesmaids, maid of honor, and bride process to the altar.

The first bridesmaid enters the sanctuary from the rear of the church at the conclusion of the wedding-march call, followed by the other bridal attendants, who should be spaced approximately twelve to twenty feet apart. It is helpful to have a "starter," to space the girls properly—this may be the pastor's wife, the florist, or the church hostess. Each girl walks slowly, in time with the music.

The bride and her father hesitate at the head of the center aisle, so that her train may be straightened by the "starter," and the organist can time the beginning with a joyous crescendo. The bride and her father, who is on her left, begin with their left feet, and keep in step. The father must remember to keep to the side of the aisle so that the bride is on his right arm. After presenting his daughter for marriage, he will be in a more convenient position to reach his seat without tripping over her train.

As the bride arrives at the chancel, she should come to the center of the aisle and stop directly in front of the minister, about two steps away. The music promptly fades out.

After these instructions are given, the participants are sent to the rooms from which they will enter, the organist is given the signal, and a walk-through rehearsal of the processional is started. Special attention should be given the ring bearer and the flower girl, if there be such. If they are a part of the party, it might be wise to have the best man responsible for the ring bearer and the maid of honor for the flower girl.

Diagrams of Arrangements

Key to Diagrams

M, minister; G, groom; BM, best man; U, ushers; BM, bridesmaids; MH, maid (or matron) of honor; FG, flower girl or pages; RB, ring bearer; BF, bride's father; B, bride.

Possible Processional Arrangements

PLAN 1

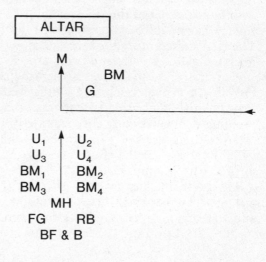

PLAN 2

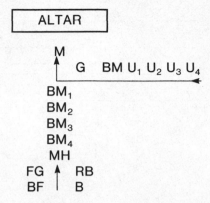

PLAN 3

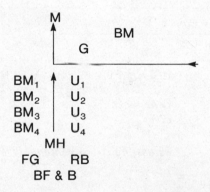

Possible Arrangements at the Chancel Steps

PLAN 1

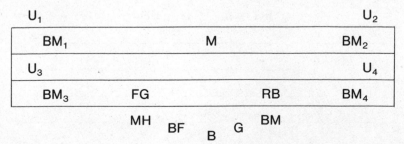

PLAN 2

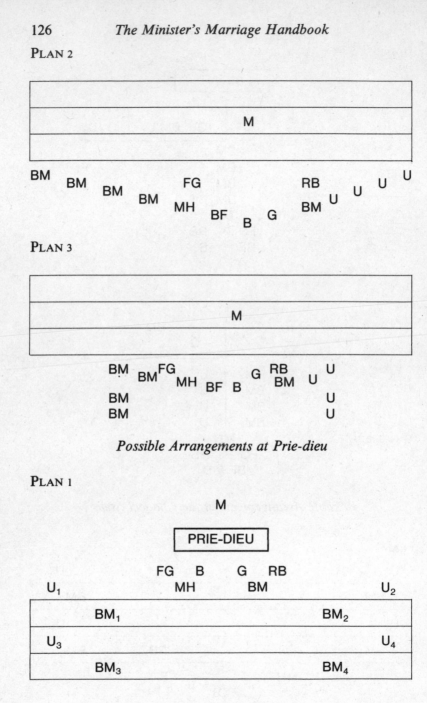

PLAN 3

Possible Arrangements at Prie-dieu

PLAN 1

PLAN 2

M

PRIE-DIEU

B   G

FG   RB

MH	BM
BM	U
BM	U

    BM   U
    BM   U

PLAN 3

M

PRIE-DIEU

B   G

MH   BM

   BM   FG   RB   U
BM   BM   U   U
BM   U

Possible Recessional Arrangements

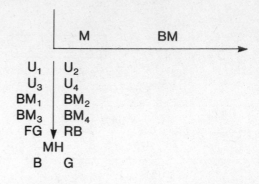

PLAN 1

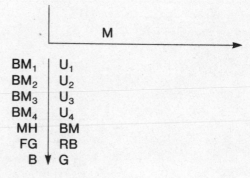

PLAN 2

Escorting Mothers Out

FIRST—BRIDE'S MOTHER | BF
BM ↓ U

SECOND—GROOM'S MOTHER | GF
GM ↓ U

Details of the Ceremony

In order for the service to proceed smoothly and to eliminate confusion, it is essential that all details be considered beforehand.

It is important to remind the participants that the wedding is a sacred worship service, to be conducted with dignity, reverence, and order. No one should chew gum. Attention should be focused upon the one officiating, with no wandering of eyes or distracting movements. During prayers, members of the wedding party bow their heads.

At the proper time, the minister asks something such as: "Who giveth this woman to be the bride of this man?" Whereupon the bride's father, with his left hand, may take her right hand, approach the minister one step, place her hand in the minister's, and say, "Her mother and I do," or "I do." For the bride's right hand to be free for this necessitates her dropping her father's arm immediately upon arrival at the chancel, and transferring her bouquet from the right to the left hand. After this he is seated by the bride's mother and next to the aisle. (The details here may vary according to the minister's wishes.) When the bride approaches the minister, she moves slightly to her left, so that as she and the groom are asked to join right hands, he steps forward to her side and stretches forth his right hand, and the minister can gently place the bride's hand on his.

It is helpful for the groom and bride to know that the wedding pledge is composed of a series of questions, so that when it is directed to each personally, they will not respond until the end. The minister should assure them that he will have an inflection in his voice. At the rehearsal it is helpful for the closing phrase to be recited, so that each will know his and her cue to answer "I will." In some ceremonies the correct response is "I do"; however, "I will" is preferred by most denominations because it carries the connotation of permanency. The answer should be given clearly.

For the ring exchange and vows, the bride and groom, maid of honor, and best man move from the chancel steps to the prie-dieu (or altar). The minister turns and takes his place behind the prie-dieu, which is the signal for the four to move forward. The groom assists the bride up the steps. They drop hands, however, upon reaching their stations, about two feet in front of the prie-dieu, so that the bride may transfer her flowers to the maid of honor at the appropriate time.

The best man has, or gets from the ring bearer, the bride's ring, and gives it to the minister when requested. The maid of honor does likewise with the groom's ring. When the rings are placed, care must be taken to put them on the proper finger of the left hand. If the bride wears gloves, the left-hand, third finger of the glove should be cut or the glove removed for the ring exchange. The bride removes her engagement ring prior to the service and wears it on her right hand. If the ring does not slip easily over the knuckle, it should be left at the knuckle for the time being, rather than struggle with it; later, it can be forced on. The bride and groom should say their vows to each other. In some ceremonies, the vows are memorized; in others, each repeats after the minister the phrases of the wedding vows. If the ring is dropped accidentally, a spare should be ready, or the best man should be alerted to retrieve it, while all retain composure.

Most formal wedding ceremonies conclude with kneeling at the prie-dieu, during which time the benediction blessing is spoken or sung. The bride kneels first, with the assistance of the groom; after she is situated, he kneels. While kneeling, the back should be erect. The groom places his left hand over the bride's right hand on the upright of the prie-dieu; they support themselves with their outside hands.

Upon the conclusion of the benediction, after the "Amen" is said, the couple rises, and they face each other and prepare to kiss. The bride's veil is lifted to the top of her head either by the maid of honor or by the groom.

Discretion, brevity, and good judgment should be used in the kiss, which is a public seal of the covenant and not a prolonged embrace of passion. A tender, brief kiss of affection is most appropriate.

As the couple turn to leave, following the kiss, the minister may, if he desires, say to the congregation: "I now present to you Mr. and Mrs. _____."

The Recessional

Following the wedding kiss, the organist begins the recessional music. The bride takes her husband's right arm, and they recess out the center aisle.

According to strictest etiquette, the maid of honor leaves alone, followed by the bridesmaids, by twos, and the groomsmen, by twos. The best man and minister then leave by the side door. The reason for this recessional order is that only the bride and groom are to be paired into a couple, and the others in the party have nothing particularly in common and may even be complete strangers. However, the general custom is for the party to leave by pairing off—the maid of honor and best man, and each bridesmaid with a groomsman.

Dismissing the Congregation

Immediately following the recessional of the wedding party, the bride's mother is ushered out. Since the father is seated next to the aisle, the usher hesitates when approaching him, so that the bride's father can get out and take one step toward the chancel while the mother steps out and takes the usher's arm. If the bride's grandmother is present, the bride's father may usher her out as he leaves. The same procedure is followed in escorting the groom's mother.

If the attendance is large, the congregation should be ushered out two rows at a time. After ushering out the bride's and groom's mothers, the two ushers come to the front and dismiss one row on each side simultaneously.

If the attendance is small, the minister remains at the priedieu until the parents are escorted out and then dismisses (with upraised hands) all of the congregation, or the head usher may come to the front of the center aisle and dismiss them with a similar gesture.

Photographs

Picture taking during the wedding ceremony is discouraged or forbidden justifiably in most churches because it is a worship service, not a performance. Often, permission is given for one photograph at the rear of the sanctuary as the bride and father begin their procession and one from the same location of the bride and groom recessing. Posing for photographs may precede the reception if no more than fifteen minutes is absorbed; if a longer time than this is needed, the guests would become tired of waiting, and the photographs should follow the reception.

Good organization, cooperation, and speed must be exercised, to eliminate the prolonged standing of the guests who await the reception.

The bride should impress upon the photographer in advance the church's policy, the time limit, and the poses desired.

Receiving Line

Everyone attending the wedding wants to have an opportunity to congratulate the couple and to wish them well. There are two ways this may be done.

The first is to have a receiving line either at the exit after the ceremony or at the entrance to the reception. The traditional receiving line starts with the bride's mother, followed by the groom's mother. However, if the reception is held in the groom's hometown, where his mother knows most of the guests, it is better for her to be first in line.

Fathers usually are not in the receiving line and mingle with the guests. However, they may be in it, if preferred, and would stand next to their wives.

The groom stands between his mother and the bride. The maid or matron of honor is next to the bride and last in line. The bridesmaids are not usually in the receiving line, rather they circulate among the guests. Young children are seldom expected to stand in the receiving line.

Some prefer not to have a receiving line. In such case the two sets of parents may station themselves at different parts of the reception room and greet guests informally. The bride and groom then circulate among the guests and strive to thank everyone for their attendance.

Guest Book

The guest book may be placed on a stand in the church's foyer or near the entrance of the receiving line at the reception. A friend of the bride or member of the family may preside there. It will be a valued memento of the occasion, and every effort should be made for every guest to sign. Usually there is a place for the officiant to sign as well.

Chapter Ten

Wedding Etiquette the Minister Should Know

The Minister's Wedding Attire

Appropriate wedding dress for the minister varies with the church tradition and possibly with the type and hour of wedding.

There is much to be said for wearing the robe vestment. Traditionally, it is distinctive for the clergy and sets one apart as the presiding person. It is tasteful and dignified and lends reverence and sacredness to the occasion. The robe is appropriate for all wedding occasions and relieves the clergyman of trying to match the attire of the male attendants. It covers the shirt, tie, and trousers, and hence is not distracting in any way.

For ministers who prefer not to wear a robe or those whose tradition forbids it, the garb should be determined by the formality and time of the wedding. A formal wedding requires formal attire—this usually means a black tuxedo, with matching accessories of black shoes, socks, and bow tie; or, it may mean a white, single-breasted jacket with black tuxedo trousers. The minister should inquire at an early wedding conference what kind of garb, including the tie, is to be worn by the male attendants; then he plans to dress accordingly.

For an informal wedding in the morning or afternoon, or one held in the parish home, the minister may wear a dark business suit with conservative tie.

133

Mature Bride's First Marriage

Simplicity and good taste are the order for the older bride's wedding, which usually is a small, informal chapel or home wedding, attended by family and close friends. She may wear white and a formal wedding dress if she chooses, but most choose a more informal style.

When Parents Are Divorced

When a daughter lives with her mother, who is divorced from her father, the invitations are sent out in the mother's name. Her present husband's name may be included, if she has remarried. Never do divorced parents send them out together. In such circumstances, it is better that the wedding be given by the mother; to do otherwise might imply that the mother had been unfit to have the custody of her daughter.

The bride's mother should be seated in the regular pew reserved for the bride's mother, with members of her family and her second husband, if she is remarried.

It is proper that the father walk up the aisle of the church with his daughter and give her away, even though the invitations are sent out by his former wife. He then takes his place in one of the pews further back on the bride's side. If remarried, he may be accompanied by his new wife. If relations are strained, some other male relative may give the bride away, or her mother might if her father is not to attend the wedding.

If the groom's parents are divorced, again, the mother and family should be given the regular pew on the groom's side of the church, and the father seated several rows behind on the same side.

Every effort should be made to make the meetings of the divorced parents friendly and not conspicuously tense. The bride or groom needs to feel that those who brought her or him into existence are on this day brought together peacefully because of their mutual concern for their offspring's happiness.

If the bride's remarried mother gives the reception, her husband acts as host, and the bride's father attends only as a guest. If the father gives the reception, and he has not remarried, he stands first in the line to receive guests. If he has remarried, his wife acts as hostess. If the bride's mother attends the reception under the latter circumstances, she is present as a guest, and should not stand at the side of her former husband or share duties as hostess.

Second Marriages

Some churches do not allow second marriages of divorced persons held in the church. There is a general relaxing of such rules, especially when a series of counseling sessions have been attended by the bride and groom. Couples usually do what they want and what will please their families and guests. However, good taste and common sense dictate respect for some guidelines.

Gift showers are not usually given for a second-time bride, though parties are permissible. Often second marriages are happier and more responsibly entered into, so it is a time for joy and celebration.

Premarital counseling is important before entering a second union because there are many potential problem areas that need to be faced. The high incidence of divorce among those going into marriage the second go-around indicates the urgent need.

If it is a second marriage for the groom but the first for the bride, plans for a beautiful wedding need not be affected.

If it is the bride's second marriage, the bride and groom should pay for the second wedding, since the parents of each assumed the respective costs for the first marriage. Usually, in such a case, the second wedding should be more modest and less elaborate than the first. If it takes place after the death of a first mate or after a divorce is granted, the more quiet and informal the wedding the better. Usually it is discreet to invite only the close relatives and friends.

Many second weddings include a private nuptial ceremony for the immediate family, which is followed by a reception, party, or dinner to which a larger number of friends and relatives is invited.

The wedding attire is dependent upon personal taste. The

bride wears nothing emblematic of virginity, such as a veil, orange blossoms, or myrtle wreath. Traditionally white has not been worn by second-time brides. This is changing somewhat as couples consider white as a symbol of the wedding rather than a symbol of the bride's purity. Sometimes off white is worn. Emily Post says white is acceptable if worn with colored accessories.

The second-time bride does not carry a bouquet. The "giving of the bride" by her father, the processional, and recessional also are eliminated.

Engagement and wedding rings from a first marriage should cease to be worn long before a second marriage. They may be kept to be given the children of the first marriage when they reach an accountable age. Or the stones may be reset in another piece of jewelry, preferably not a ring.

Unless the family of her first husband deeply disapproves of her second marriage, a widowed bride sends them invitations to her second wedding.

Very young children of a first marriage perhaps should not attend the second marriage of either parent, yet as a general rule, older children of a first marriage should be invited to attend unless they are bitter and do not like the spouse. A parent rushing to remarry needs to confide in and to seek approval from the children. Unless it is an obvious mismating, with ulterior motives, children should give their blessings and very best wishes. If children of a previous marriage persistently resent the proposed new marriage, it is advisable to marry with only the necessary legal witnesses present.

When Remarrying Former Spouse

When persons formerly divorced wish to be reunited to each other in marriage, no formal announcements should be sent out. However, it is a time of celebration. Friends and relatives are informed by letter or telephone. Often the children are included in the happy reunion.

Persons Living Together

Should a couple who have been living together be married in the church or by a minister? Though such live-in practice is contrary to the moral standards of most churches, yet most will rejoice that the couple have come at last to the commitment included in marriage. Each church and pastor will need to make his own policy. I suspect the decision would hinge upon the attitudes of the couple, the view of marriage held, and the premarital-counseling sessions.

If the pastor and the church can avoid the image of "condoning habitation without benefit of marriage," can rejoice in their marriage as with any other, and can convey the deeper meanings of commitment, then celebrate the marriage and be glad!

When the Bride's Mother Gives Her Away

If the bride's father is dead, the bride's mother may give her away, if a brother, an uncle, or some other male relative hasn't been selected for the honor. There are several ways this may be done—the bride's mother may walk down the aisle with her daughter, but not, of course, with the bride on her arm; the bride may walk in the processional with her brother or other male relative, her mother joining as she reaches the left front pew; sometimes the bride walks alone in the processional, and her mother joins her as she reaches her mother's pew; a male relative may escort the bride to the chancel steps, and, when the clergyman asks who is to give the bride away, the mother nods or stands to say "I do" from her traditional place or, just before the words are to be spoken, is escorted to the chancel by the best man, who steps down for the gesture. The latter is necessary only in those ceremonies (Episcopalian, for example) where the one who "gives the bride away" actually places her hand in the minister's.[1]

Postponing a Wedding or Recalling Invitations

When death occurs in the immediate family of the bride or groom, it is proper for the wedding to be postponed. If the death is of a very old person—a grandmother or grandfather—who has been ill, postponement is rarely called for. The action to be taken depends upon the feelings of the persons involved and the traveling distances required.

If the decision is made to postpone the wedding or to recall invitations for this or any other reason, the guests should be notified by telephone, wire, or, if time permits, by printed cards in the same style as the invitations.

The Double Wedding

Occasionally, sisters, cousins, or just close friends wish to marry at the same time in a double wedding. This can be most meaningful, dramatic, and impressive. The double wedding need not be formal, nor must participants dress alike.

In the double wedding, each bride and each groom usually have separate attendants, with the same number involved and harmonizing color schemes. Sometimes sisters have the same attendants. The brides may act as maid and matron of honor for each other, and the grooms as best men for each other.

The ushers of both groups must be dressed identically, even when the bridesmaids' costumes differ for each bride. The only time when ushers may be dressed differently is when civilians and military men serve together. In a double wedding, all the ushers are paired according to height in the processional.

If the church has two interior aisles leading to the chancel, each bridal party may use a separate aisle, timing the entrance and exit together. The mothers of the brides and grooms are escorted up the respective aisles by ushers in the usual way just before the ceremony begins. The grooms' mothers are seated in the section to the right of the aisles; the brides' mothers are seated in the section to the left of the aisles.

If the church has only a center aisle, with no other interior aisles, then the procession is up the center aisle. Both grooms' mothers are seated in the section to the right of the aisle, with the mother of the groom of the older bride using the front row, and the other groom's mother the next row. The brides' mothers are seated in the section to the left of the aisle, with the older bride's mother in the front row and the other mother in the second row. The party of the older bride processes first, followed by the party of the younger bride. If the girls are sisters, the father escorts the older girl, and a brother or other male relative escorts her sister. In the recessional, the elder bride, who has married first, leads down the chancel steps with her groom, and is followed by the younger bride with her groom. The attendants follow in the proper order, those of the first bride first, or paired with those of the second bride if an equal number makes it possible. Otherwise, they leave as they arrived.

The Home Wedding

The home is a frequent setting for a wedding. If the wedding is large, the largest room is cleared, an altar is improvised at some focal point as far from the entrance as possible, and sections for the parents and relatives are roped off. When there is a staircase, the bride descends it when the wedding march is played. Otherwise, the bridal party congregates outside the entrance of the room before the music begins.

If the wedding is small, there may be no music at all, with participants dressed informally. The clergyman leads the wedding party to the place prepared for the ceremony.

A reception usually is given at a home wedding. It may be in the same room as that in which the wedding takes place, in the garden, or on a porch. A large table is usually moved against a wall, and set with the wedding cake as the central theme.

A wedding may take place out of doors if the climate is sufficiently dependable and if alternative arrangements have been made in case of inclement weather.

Receiving at a Home Wedding

At a home wedding, there is no recessional unless a formal receiving line is to form elsewhere in the house or in the garden. Where there are many guests and space is limited, the receiving line, if there is to be one, is best located in a small room such as a hall or dining room with both exit and entrance to facilitate the steady flow of traffic. Guests should be able to pass on into a larger area, where they may congregate and have refreshments. In simple home weddings, it is usual for the bride and groom merely to turn around at the altar after the benediction and kiss, to receive congratulations.

The Wedding in a Clergyman's Family

A clergyman, like any other groom, is married in the church of his bride by her own clergyman. If she belongs to the church he serves, then they may be married there by some other clergyman of his faith—his superior, a friend, or a clergyman from a neighboring parish or congregation. Occasionally, if he has an assistant, the couple is married by him. However, it is usual for a minister of his own rank or higher to perform the ceremony.

A clergyman may announce his forthcoming marriage from the pulpit on a Sunday and invite the congregation to attend, if the marriage is to take place in his house of worship. Such a procedure, though it is followed occasionally, risks the exclusion of members who did not attend services on the day the announcement was made. The sending of individual invitations, using the entire church mailing list or an invitation in the church paper that is sent to all the parish families are more correct and effective procedures. When the bride comes from a distance to be married in her husband's church, the people of the congregation might give the reception, especially if the couple's joint circumstances are modest.

A minister is usually given the honor of conducting the ceremony for his own son in the bride's place of worship, with the bride's clergyman assisting. The clergyman's congregation does not usually expect to be invited en masse if the distance for the wedding is great, though various officers of the congregation might well be included in the invitation list.

When the daughter of a clergyman marries, she may be escorted to the altar by her father, with a pastor friend conducting the service until after the point where the father "gives the bride away"; then the father may conduct the remainder of the service. An alternative is for the bride to be escorted by an older brother, a brother-in-law, an uncle, or a family friend; after accompanying her to the altar, the escort may give her away, or he may take a place in a pew on the bride's side while the bride's father steps forward to give her away.

Wedding Anniversaries

Here is a list of the type of gifts traditionally given on each anniversary:

First—paper
Second—cotton
Third—leather
Fourth—linen (silk)
Fifth—wood
Sixth—iron
Seventh—wool and copper
Eighth—bronze
Ninth—pottery (china)
Tenth—tin (aluminum)
Eleventh—steel
Twelfth—silk

Thirteenth—lace
Fourteenth—ivory
Fifteenth—crystal
Twentieth—china
Twenty-fifth—silver
Thirtieth—pearl
Thirty-fifth—coral
Fortieth—ruby
Forty-fifth—sapphire
Fiftieth—gold
Fifty-fifth—emerald
Sixtieth—diamond

Chapter Eleven

Nonceremony Prayers and Toasts

Wedding Prayers
For the Minister's Final Counseling Session

Gracious God, You have kindled within _____ and _____ a fire of love for each other. We have been glad for these times together surveying ourselves—our natures, the views of marriage, the expectations, the strengths and weaknesses, the areas of chief concern, and the meaning of love.

Grant, O Lord, that each may have a clearer understanding of self, a greater sensitivity to the other, a deepened respect, and a realistic view of love. Help each to have a total inward concurrence about marrying the other, not with fingers crossed, but with a lifelong commitment. If there is hesitation, let them be courageously honest with each other before saying, "I do." As they prepare to launch their lives together in faith, give them the capacity to transcend minor irritations, the discipline to adjust harmoniously to each other, the humor and appreciation to bring out the very best in each other, and the will to keep the sacred vows.

Grant that the fires of love may burn with increasing intensity until it fuses their lives into perfect oneness, through the Spirit of Jesus Christ, our Lord. *Amen.*

For the Wedding Rehearsal

God and Father of all, You have ordained marriage for the happiness and welfare of human beings and for the procreation and development of the race. Look with favor upon this union of _____ and _____.

They have grown to love, trust, and cherish each other; now they come to make public what they have conveyed in private and to formally pledge themselves to each other in holy matrimony.

O Lord, help us who share in this high experience to realize its sacredness. We feel it a unique honor. So give to each of us a sense of personal responsibility in our assignment, that the wedding will proceed orderly, joyfully, reverently and will honor You, in whose presence we live and in whose name we pray. *Amen.*

The Rehearsal Dinner

Eternal God, the Creator to whom we owe the gift of life; we thank You for the "ties that bind our hearts in love." We thank You for this happy hour that brings us together as family and friends of _____ and _____.

As we share this food, O Lord, bless it to our strength and health. As we enjoy fellowship, O Lord, bless it to our mutual enrichment. In honoring this couple we also honor their families and the larger family of Christ's new humanity, in whose name we pray. *Amen.*

A Bride's Wedding-Day Prayer

(*Copy may be given to bride at rehearsal.*)

Gracious God, my heart is filled with rapture and gratitude for the one who seems worthy of my deepest commitment and companionship.

Today, as we are united in holy matrimony, I thank You for the teachings that have guided my life, the love that has surrounded me, the providence that directed my decisions, and my parents and friends who share this high moment.

Help me to prove to be a loving sweetheart, faithful helpmate, and congenial companion. May my voice not lose the tender tone it has known in courtship's smiling days. Grant to me, O Lord, the wisdom to make home the best loved of all places, the health to fulfill my duties cheerfully, and the grace and disposition to meet constructively the problems and irritations that will arise.

If it be Your will, grant to me the privilege of parenthood and the virtues of good motherhood.

When all my youthful charms have vanished, and the lines of care and age have diminished physical attraction, may we be found walking hand in hand by the bond of Your eternal love, through Jesus Christ. *Amen.*

A Groom's Wedding-Day Prayer

(*Copy may be given to groom at rehearsal.*)

My God and Father, how marvelous is Your plan for the fulfillment of personality and life. I thank You for the one who has grown to love me and who this day gives herself to my keeping. Together may we grow in love and affection and mutuality, until two hearts beat as one.

O Lord, grant that I may be worthy of her trust, love, and devotion. Fill me with the Christ-like spirit of thoughtfulness, unselfishness, self-control, dependability, and understanding that will make for a happy and abiding marriage. May no deeds or words of mine dim her eyes with tears of grief.

Give me the grace to accept her parents as my own and to be worthy of their acceptance of me. If it be possible, bless our union with the gift of children and us with the wisdom of responsible parents.

May the years together bring to full blossom the love of our hearts, faithful service in Your Kingdom, and the glory of Your Holy Name. *Amen.*

Newlyweds' Prayer

(*To be used as a good-night devotional on the wedding day.*)

O God, we will wonder no more that this day has been different for us from all the other days. There has been a light in the air, a glory in the sky, and a glamour on human faces, and we give You thanks.

We thank You for the people who have made the day so good; for our parents' self-forgetful service; for the companions of our youth who have shared the joy and the work of the day; for the sympathetic and gracious goodwill of the minister; and for all good wishes from sincere and loving hearts.

We give You thanks for each other. Grant us someday to know fully the mystery of Your plan by which these lives of ours have moved to seek each other out above all others to find completion. Reveal increasingly the beauty of our marriage vows.

So, O Lord, we go forward seeking Your guidance and Your will. Hallow every hour of our united lives. In Jesus' name. *Amen.*

Anniversary Prayers[1]

General Anniversary

PRAYER

> God of our years,
> you created man and woman
> to love each other
> in the bond of marriage.
> Bless and strengthen (*name*) and (*name*).
>
> May their marriage become an increasingly
> more perfect sign of the union between
> Christ and his Church
> We ask this through our Lord Jesus Christ,
> your Son,
> who lives and reigns with you and the
> Holy Spirit,
> one God, for ever and ever. *Amen.*

PRAYER AFTER COMMUNION

> Lord, you give us food and drink from
> heaven.
> Bless (*name*) and (*name*) on their anniversary.
> Let their love grow stronger
> that they may find within themselves

a greater peace and joy.
Bless their home
that all who come to it in need
may find in it an example of goodness
and a source of comfort.
We ask this through Christ our
      Lord. *Amen.*

Twenty-fifth Anniversary

PRAYER

Lord of Life,
you have blessed and sustained (*name*) and
    (*name*) in the bond of marriage.
Continue to increase their love
throughout the joys and sorrows of life,
and help them to grow in holiness
    all their days.
Grant this through our Lord Jesus Christ,
    your Son,
who lives and reigns with you and the
    Holy Spirit,
one God, for ever and ever. *Amen.*

PRAYER AFTER COMMUNION

Eternal God,
you bring (*name*) and (*name*) [and
their children and friends] together
at the table of your family.
Help them grow in love and unity,
that they may rejoice together
in the wedding feast of heaven.
Grant this through Christ our Lord. *Amen.*

Fiftieth Anniversary

PRAYER

Lord our God,
bless (*name*) and (*name*).

We thank you for their long
and happy marriage,
[for the children they have
brought into the world,]
and for all the good they have done.
As you blessed the love of their youth,
continue to bless their life together
with gifts of peace and joy.
We ask this through our Lord Jesus Christ,
your Son,
who lives and reigns with you and the
Holy Spirit,
one God, for ever and ever. *Amen.*

PRAYER AFTER COMMUNION

Lord,
as we gather at the table of your Son,
bless (*name*) and (*name*)
on their wedding anniversary.
Watch over them in the coming years,
and bring them to the feast of eternal life.
Grant this through Christ our Lord. *Amen.*

Wedding Toasts

The toast is an ancient French custom. A piece of toasted crouton was placed in the bottom of a beverage glass, filled with drink. One then drank the beverage to get to the "toast."

It has become traditional at weddings to propose sentiments and best wishes to the bride and groom with the toast.

Toasts can be done with whatever beverage one is drinking—water, grape juice, punch, or champagne, depending upon the wishes of the bride and groom and the individuals. The importance of the toast is not the beverage; it is the spoken words.

Toasts for Engagement-Announcement Party

If there is an engagement dinner or party, the bride's father makes the engagement announcement and then proposes the first toast to his daughter and his future son-in-law. The groom responds with a toast to his bride and her parents, expressing his appreciation.

SUGGESTIONS FOR FATHER

I propose this toast to our daughter _____ and our future son-in-law _____. May the joy of this night be yours throughout all your days; may no dark clouds of sordidness obscure the clear light of your devotion. May no gray disenchantment ever have power to destroy your dreams.

SUGGESTIONS FOR THE GROOM

Out of all the persons I have met, I have chosen _____ to be my wife. I love her. I appreciate you, her parents, for your acceptance and love of me. I promise to do my best to be an honorable husband to her and to make you proud of me as a son. I propose this toast to my bride in the paraphrased words of an old English toast: Love, be true to you; Life, be dear to you; Health, stay close to you; Joy, draw near to you. Fortune, find what you can for us; Search your treasure house through for us. Follow our footsteps wherever we go. And keep me always your lover.

Toasts for the Rehearsal Dinner

At the rehearsal dinner, the father of the groom proposes the first toast to the bride and groom, followed by other family members and wedding party participants. It is appropriate for the minister to propose a toast also, if he wishes, perhaps after all the others have done so.

SUGGESTIONS FOR THE GROOM'S FATHER

We want to thank each of you for your participation in this high moment in our family and for your coming to this dinner. I propose this toast to our son and our future daughter-in-law _____. May each of you have the qualities of personality, the virtues of spirit, and the strength of character that will make you loyal, lovable, and unselfish marriage partners.

SUGGESTIONS FOR THE MINISTER

May you be like two trees, though separated by their plant-ing, they grow tall and straight, stretching toward the sun, overlapping their branches, intertwining their roots. Together they sway in the wind, sing in the sun, dance in the breeze. They stand tall, side by side, protecting each other from the storms. Saplings spring up in the shadows. Cut deeply in the bark of each, which time can never efface, are the tender words, "I love you."

So may it be with you, dear hearts.

Or

May you have enough success to expand your opportunities for doing good, enough failure to keep your hands clenched in God's, enough tears to keep you tender, enough hurt to make you compassionate, enough joy to keep you radiant, and enough faith to ever look to tomorrow.

Toasts for Wedding Reception or Dinner

At the wedding reception, it is appropriate to have a toast to the newly married. The best man proposes the first toast to the bride and groom. He may be the only one to do so, or other members of the wedding party may join in proposing toasts.

If the bride and groom are seated at a dinner when the toasts are proposed to them, they remain seated and all others stand.

SUGGESTED TOAST FOR THE BEST MAN

May your marriage be a happy, enduring, and thrilling adventure.

Chapter Twelve

Traditional Church Wedding Services

The wedding ceremony should be set in a worship framework, with appropriate music content. The traditional and generally accepted wedding service plan used in most churches is as follows:

Prelude music
Seating of guests
Lighting of candles
Groom's parents seated
Bride's mother seated
Aisle cloth unrolled
Vocal music
The wedding processional
The marriage ceremony
The wedding recessional
Bride's parents ushered out
Groom's parents ushered out
Congregation dismissed

Slight alterations are often made in this procedure, in accordance with local policy, practice, or desire.

A Nondenominational
Form for Solemnization of Marriage

When the persons to be married have come before the minister, he shall say:

We are met in the presence of God to unite this man and this woman by the sacred ties of matrimony. Let us pray:

God, be merciful unto us and bless us, and cause His face to shine upon us, through Jesus Christ our Lord. Amen.

Becoming more sacred in the estimation of men, marriage has existed from the beginning of human history. It has the sanction of heaven, having been instituted by God and honored by Jesus of Nazareth, and it should have the approbation of all. From it, founded in reason, loyal, just and pure, have sprung all the sweet charities of family and home, and the uplifting and refining influences that flow out from them.

Those who take its vows are brought into the closest and most sacred of human relationships. Their lives are blended into one as the waters of confluent streams are mingled, and thenceforth, they must share the joys and sorrows of life. And from this close and intimate relationship spring obligations of the most solemn and lasting character. The husband is under obligations to throw around the wife his protecting care, to shield her from the rough storms of the world, to cling to her with unfaltering fidelity, to cherish her with unfailing affection, and to guard her happiness with unceasing vigilance. And the wife is under obligation to love and cherish her husband, to honor and sustain him, and to be true to him in all ways. Each is under obligation to fulfill the love ordained of God as recorded in 1 Corinthians 13.

"This love of which I speak is slow to lose patience—it looks for a way of being constructive. It is not possessive: it is neither anxious to impress nor does it cherish inflated ideas of its own importance. Love has good manners and does not pursue selfish advantage. It is not touchy. It does not compile statistics of evil or gloat over the wickedness of other people. On the contrary, it is glad with all good men when Truth prevails. Love knows no limit to its endurance, no end to its trust, no fading of its hope; it can outlast anything. It is, in fact, the one thing that still stands when all else has fallen" (1 Corinthians 13:4–7 PHILLIPS).

Then the minister shall say: Who giveth this woman to be the bride of this man?

Then the father, or whoever takes his place, shall answer: I do. (Or, Her mother and I do.)

And now, if you, knowing of nothing either legal or moral to forbid your union in marriage, wish to take its vows and assume its obligations, indicate that wish by joining your right hands.

Their hands being clasped, the minister shall ask the man:

Will you, _____, have this woman _____, whose hand you hold to be your wedded wife, and solemnly promise that you will loyally fulfill your obligations as her husband to protect her, honor her, love her, and cherish her in adversity as well as in prosperity and keep yourself unto her alone, so long as you both shall live?

The man shall answer: I will.

Then the minister shall ask the woman: Will you, _____, have this man _____, whose hand you hold to be your wedded husband and solemnly promise that you will be unto him a tender, loving, and true wife through sunshine and shadow alike, and be faithful to him so long as you both shall live?

The woman shall answer: I will.

Let us pray: Almighty God, heavenly Father of mankind, whose nature is love: Look with favor upon this man and this woman who desire now to make their vows before Thee. We are grateful for the families that have reared them to maturity, the church which has nurtured them with ideals, and the Providence which has led them to this happy and holy altar of marriage. Grant this to be more than an outward union, but rather the blending of hearts and spirits and purposes. Bless each with the inward qualities of loyalty, honor, purity, self-control, trust, cooperation, and forgiveness, that they may keep faithfully this holy convenant, and may live together all their days in true love and perfect peace, through Jesus Christ the Master of the art of living, and our Saviour. Amen.

Then shall they loose their hands and move to the altar, and the minister shall say: We read in the old story that when God made a covenant with Noah, He set a bow in the cloud as a token thereof, and said, "I will look upon it, that I may remember the everlasting covenant." From this we may learn that it is well for us, when we enter into solemn agreement one with another, to set apart some reminder of what we have promised. As tokens of your marriage covenant, you have each selected a ring of gold.

Here the ring (or rings) shall be given to the minister and he shall say: Gold, precious among metals, fittingly represents the precious ties that unite husband and wife. These (this) rings (ring), endless until broken by outside forces, are (is a) fit symbols (symbol) of the unbroken partnership of marriage which should continue until broken by death. Let them (it) be unto you constant reminders (a constant reminder) of your obligations to each other, and mute incentives (a mute incentive) to their fulfillment.

Then the minister shall say to the man: Forasmuch as the husband imparts to his wife his name and receives her into his care and keeping, I give you this ring. Put it upon the wedding finger of your bride, and say to her these words: I, _____, give this ring to you, _____, and by this act declare, in the presence of these witnesses, that I take you to be my beloved wife; that I will be unto you a faithful husband until death shall part us.

Then the minister shall say to the woman: Take the ring which you have selected put it upon the wedding finger of your bridegroom, and say to him these words: I, _____, give this ring to you, _____, (if single ring ceremony, the woman will say: I, _____, receive this ring from you, _____,) and thus declare, in the presence of these witnesses that you are the husband of my choice, that I will be faithful to you until death shall part us.

Thus, you are to wear these rings (this ring) as the enclosing bond of reverence and trust. You both are to fulfill the perfect circle of duty that makes you one. As you hope for happiness in your married life, I charge you to be true to the vows you have taken. With your marriage, you begin life under new conditions and with larger responsibilities; and it is only by faithfully performing the duties and fulfilling the obligations of the new relation that true and lasting happiness can be found.

Forasmuch as you, _____, and you, _____, have openly declared your wishes to be united in marriage, and in the presence of God, and before these witnesses have pledged love and fidelity each to the other, and have confirmed the same by each giving and receiving a ring, and by joining hands, I, as a minister of Christ's Church and legally authorized so to do by the State of _____, pronounce now that you are Husband and Wife.

To the man: Guard well this woman who now commits herself to your keeping, and strive so to live that no word or deed of yours shall cloud her brow with sorrow or dim her eyes with tears or grief. *To the woman:* And you strive to retain by your virtues the heart you have won by your graces. *To both:* Let not your voices lose the tender tones of affection. Let not "your eyes forget the gentle ray they wore in courtship's smiling day." So you will find in your union an unfailing source of joy, being one in name, one in aim, and one in happy destiny together.

Let us kneel: Entreat me not to leave you or to return from following you; for where you go I will go, and where you lodge I will lodge; your people shall be my people, and your God my God (Ruth 1:16 RSV).

The Lord bless you and keep you; the Lord make His face to shine upon you, and be gracious unto you; the Lord lift up His countenance upon you and give you peace. Amen.[1]

A Form for Solemnization of Matrimony According to the Book of Common Prayer

At the day and time appointed for solemnization of Matrimony, the Persons to be married shall come into the body of the Church, or shall be ready in some proper house, with their friends and neighbors; and there standing together, the Man on the right hand, and the Woman on the left, the Minister shall say,

Dearly beloved, we are gathered together here in the sight of God, and in the face of this company, to join together this Man and this Woman in holy Matrimony; which is an honourable estate, instituted of God, signifying unto us the mystical union that is betwixt Christ and his Church: which holy estate Christ adorned and beautified with his presence and first miracle that he wrought in Cana of Galilee, and is commended of Saint Paul to be honourable among all men: and therefore is not by any to be entered into unadvisedly or lightly; but reverently, discreetly, advisedly, soberly, and in the fear of God. Into this holy estate these two persons present come now to be joined. If any man can show just cause, why they may not lawfully be joined together, let him now speak, or else hereafter for ever hold his peace.

And also speaking unto the Persons who are to be married, he shall say,

I require and charge you both, as ye will answer at the dreadful day of judgment when the secrets of all hearts shall be disclosed, that if either of you know any impediment, why ye may not be lawfully joined together in Matrimony, ye do now confess it. For be ye well assured, that if any persons are joined together otherwise than as God's Word doth allow, their marriage is not lawful.

The Minister, if he shall have reason to doubt of the lawfulness of the proposed Marriage, may demand sufficient surety for his indemnification: but if no impediment shall be alleged, or suspected, the Minister shall say to the Man,

_____, wilt thou have this Woman to be thy wedded wife, to live together after God's ordinance in the holy estate of Matrimony? Wilt thou love her, comfort her, honour, and keep her in sickness and in health; and, forsaking all others, keep thee only unto her, so long as ye both shall live?

The Man shall answer, I will.

Then shall the Minister say unto the Woman,

_____, wilt thou have this man to thy wedded husband, to live together after God's ordinance in the holy estate of Matrimony? Wilt thou love him, comfort him, honour, and keep him in sickness and in health; and, forsaking all others, keep thee only unto him, so long as ye both shall live?

The Woman shall answer, I will.

Then shall the Minister say, Who giveth this Woman to be married to this Man?

Then shall they give their troth to each other in this manner. The Minister, receiving the Woman at her father's or friend's hands, shall cause the Man with his right hand to take the Woman by her right hand, and to say after him as followeth.

I, _____, take thee, _____, to be my wedded Wife, to have

and to hold from this day forward, for better for worse, for richer for poorer, in sickness and in health, to love and to cherish, till death us do part, according to God's holy ordinance; and thereto I plight thee my troth.

Then shall they loose their hands; and the Woman with her right hand taking the Man by his right hand, shall likewise say after the Minister,

I, _____, take thee, _____, to be my wedded Husband, to have and to hold from this day forward, for better for worse, for richer for poorer, in sickness and in health, to love and to cherish, till death us do part, according to God's holy ordinance; and thereto I give thee my troth.

Then shall they again loose their hands; and the Man shall give unto the Woman a Ring on this wise: the Minister taking the Ring shall deliver it unto the Man, to put it upon the fourth finger of the Woman's left hand. And the Man holding the Ring there, and taught by the Minister, shall say,

With this Ring I thee wed: In the Name of the Father, and of the Son, and of the Holy Ghost. Amen.

And, before delivering the Ring to the Man, the Minister may say as followeth.

Bless, O Lord, this Ring, that he who gives it and she who wears it may abide in thy peace, and continue in thy favour, unto their life's end; through Jesus Christ our Lord. Amen.

Then, the Man leaving the Ring upon the fourth finger of the Woman's left hand, the Minister shall say,

Let us pray.

Then shall the Minister and the People, still standing, say the Lord's Prayer.

Our Father, who art in heaven, Hallowed be thy name. Thy kingdom come. Thy will be done, On earth as it is in heaven. Give us this day our daily bread. And forgive us our trespasses, As we forgive those who trespass against us. And lead us not into temptation, But deliver us from evil. For thine is the kingdom, and the power, and the glory for ever and ever. Amen.

Then shall the Minister add,

O eternal God, Creator and Preserver of all mankind, Giver of all spiritual grace, the Author of everlasting life; Send thy blessing upon these thy servants, this man and this woman,

whom we bless in thy Name; that they, living faithfully together, may surely perform and keep the vow and covenant
betwixt them made, (whereof this Ring given and received is a
token and pledge), and may ever remain in perfect love and
peace together, and live according to thy laws; through Jesus
Christ our Lord. Amen.

The Minister may add one or both of the following prayers.

O Almighty God, Creator of mankind, who only art the
well-spring of life; Bestow upon these thy servants, if it be thy
will, the gift and heritage of children; and grant that they may
see their children brought up in thy faith and fear, to the honour and glory of thy Name; through Jesus Christ our Lord.
Amen.

O God, who hast so consecrated the state of Matrimony that
in it is represented the spiritual marriage and unity betwixt
Christ and his Church; Look mercifully upon these thy servants, that they may love, honour, and cherish each other, and
so live together in faithfulness and patience, in wisdom and
true godliness, that their home may be a haven of blessing and
of peace; through the same Jesus Christ our Lord, who liveth
and reigneth with thee and the Holy Spirit ever, one God,
world without end. Amen.

Then shall the Minister join their right hands together, and say,

Those whom God hath joined together let no man put asunder.

Then shall the Minister speak unto the company.

Forasmuch as _____ and _____ have consented together
in holy wedlock, and have witnessed the same before God and
this company, and thereto have given and pledged their troth,
each to the other, and have declared the same by giving and
receiving a Ring, and by joining hands; I pronounce that they
are Man and Wife, In the Name of the Father, and of the Son,
and of the Holy Ghost. Amen.

*The Man and Wife kneeling, the Minister shall add this Bless-
ing.*

God the Father, God the Son, God the Holy Ghost, bless,
preserve and keep you; the Lord mercifully with his favour
look upon you, and fill you with all spiritial benediction and
grace; that ye may so live together in this life, that in the world
to come ye may have life everlasting. Amen.[2]

A Community or Congregational
Marriage Service

Coming as they do to dedicate themselves unto God, and with His eternal help to fashion their house into a home, the hearth into an altar, their family into a unit of His kingdom; and to achieve within their love the very hint of eternity, _____ and _____ come seeking the sacrament of holy marriage.

Let us pray: O Thou infinite Father, bless these who come here in this high moment of their lives together. We thank Thee for all of the rich values which have flowed into them from those who loved them and nurtured them and pointed them to the way of life. We thank Thee that Thou has hidden within them the dream of a great love, and that now Thou wilt help them fashion it into a home that shall endure. We thank Thee for the values they have found by their own striving. And now as they make their promises to each other, may they make them with the deepest insight into their meaning and with their fullest sincerity. And do grant unto them the gift of a great love, and the vision of the strength to build it with Christ as the living presence, into a home that will glorify Him, for in His name we pray. Amen.

I charge you both, as you stand in the presence of God, to remember that love and loyalty alone will avail as the foundations of a happy and enduring home. If the solemn vows which you are about to make be kept permanent, and if steadfastly you seek to do the will of your Heavenly Father, your life will be full of peace and joy, and the home which you are establishing will abide through every change.

I charge you both to grow to that place where each gets major satisfaction from giving peace and happiness to the other.

If you desire this new estate to be permanent, then cherish the vision of your first love. . . . Let it not be tarnished by the common events. Believe in this ideal you both share; it is binding; it is inviolate and in all human relations it is the final truth.

And I charge you further, by God's grace, ever to be true to the words of one who said:

How do I love thee? Let me count the ways.
I love thee to the depth and breadth and height
My soul can reach. . . .

I love thee to the level of everyday's
Most quiet need, by sun and candle-light.
I love thee freely, as men strive for Right;
I love thee purely, as they turn from Praise.

. . . I love thee with the breath,
Smiles, tears, of all my life!—and, if God choose,
I shall but love thee better after death.

Elizabeth Barrett Browning,
Sonnets From the Portuguese

_____, do you take _____ to be your wedded wife, and in the presence of all these witnesses do you vow that you will do everything in your power to make your love for her a growing part of your life? Will you continue to feed it from day to day and week to week and year to year from the best resources of your living? Will you stand by her in sickness or in health, in poverty or in wealth, and will you shun all others and keep yourself to her alone so long as you both shall live?

Response:
I will.
Who gives _____ in marriage?
Do you have some vows of your love to pledge to each other?

The Groom:
I, _____, take thee, _____, to be my wedded wife, to have and to hold from this day forward, in sickness or in health, in poverty or in wealth; to love and to cherish so long as we both shall live. To this I pledge thee my faith.

The Bride:
I, _____, take thee, _____, to be my wedded husband, to have and to hold from this day forward, in sickness or in health, in poverty or in wealth; to love and to cherish so long as we both shall live. To this I pledge thee my faith.

The Groom:
With this ring I thee wed, in the name of the Father, and of the Son, and of the Holy Spirit.

The Bride:
I receive this ring as a token of my love, in the name of the Father, and of the Son, and of the Holy Spirit.
Minister:
Bless him who gives this ring and her who receives it that both may go forth with Thee as guide and ever live in Thy loving favor.
Let us kneel:

Love through eternity endures,
   For God is Love and Love is God,
      Thank God for love—His first, then yours.

Forasmuch as _____ and _____ have consented together in holy wedlock, and have witnessed the same before God and this company and have pledged their faith and love to each other, and have declared the same by joining hands, and by the giving and receiving of a ring, I pronounce that they are husband and wife. Those whom God hath joined together, let no man put asunder. In the name of the Father, and of the Son, and of the Holy Spirit. Amen.

And now may the courage of the early morning's dawning, and the strength of the eternal hills, and the peace of the evening's ending and the love of God be in your hearts now and forevermore. Amen.[3]

Wedding Worship Service

Some churches follow a form for the wedding not unlike the traditional order for Sunday morning worship. There is much to commend this increasingly used plan, because the wedding service is not entertainment. It is worship.

Primary attention is focused on God. The service proceeds in a manner similar to a regular worship service. A bulletin, much like the guide for a formal morning worship service, is presented to those attending.

Prelude Recital

"Rejoice Greatly, O my Soul!"—Karg-Elert
"Jesu, Joy of Man's Desiring"—Bach

"From God I Ne'er Will Turn Me"—Buxtehude
"Suite Gothique"—Boellmann
"O Perfect Love"—Barnby

OPENING HYMN

"Love Divine"—Zundel (*Mothers are escorted during the singing, congregation standing.*)

Call to Worship

We are met here to present _____ and _____ before God to be united in marriage, in accord with the agelong truth, verified by experience, "It is not good that the man should be alone" (Genesis 2:18 RSV), "Therefore, a man leaves his father and his mother, and cleaves to his wife, and they become one flesh" (Genesis 2:24 RSV).

Invocation Prayer

O God, who alone unites persons in holy bonds of covenant, without whose Spirit there is no abiding unity: be present in the inner being of these who desire to be married, and among these whose sacred responsibility it is to give or withhold approval—in the Spirit of Christ, the Lord, Amen.

PROCESSIONAL

"Trumpet Voluntary in D"—Purcell (*Wedding party proceeds to bottom of chancel steps.*)

Statement to congregation: We are gathered to perform a ceremony of holy matrimony.

Old Testament lesson: Ruth 1:16

Solo or anthem: "O Perfect Love"
New Testament lesson: 1 Corinthians 13:4–7

Witness to the word: The minister, in a brief witness, may speak of the significance of marriage in the Christian tradition.

The Meditation Concerning Marriage

Of all the human events, none more easily becomes an occasion for rejoicing than does marriage. Even the dullest person alive can hardly fail to have a sense of wonder as he sees a man and woman take their places before an altar and pledge their lifelong devotion to each other.

Science and art are efforts to find unity in diversity . . . but marriage not only discovers unity, but undertakes to create unity. Two lives, belonging to different sexes, and often with widely different biological backgrounds, come together in the sight of God and before their friends to inaugurate something never seen in the world before—their particular combination of inheritance and their particular union of personalities. They join their destinies in such a manner that sorrow for one will be sorrow for the other and good fortune for one will be good fortune for the other. Marriage has a mystical quality because it combines the flesh and spirit in remarkable unity, the closest physical intimacy that is possible. Moreover, the normal expected result of their union will be the coming into the world of new persons, who, apart from this union, would never have been granted the possibility of existence.

Marriage, then, is a sharing in the entire creative process and a window through which the meaning of human existence shines with unusual brilliance.

The Charge to the Congregation

True marriage can never be private or secret, because it has a public character. Not only on their wedding day, but in its entire course, it is a public affair. The community has a stake in this creative union and its offspring, and deserves the joy of participation. The community and families involved come today to give symbolic approval and blessing to your union. What happens at the altar is the stamp of approval of the Christian community. The miracle happens, not at the altar, but when you two people realize that the fulness of life for you involves a complete unity of destiny. This religious ceremony is designed so that you may make vows of lifelong fidelity, in the presence of those whose approbation and blessing you seek.

The Symbolic Approval

Now who will, in behalf of the families and their beloved community, give the stamp of approval for this woman _____ to become the wife of this man _____.

FATHER OF THE BRIDE

I do.

The Declaration of Intention

(*Traditionally, this was performed on the church steps at the time of the engagement announcement. Later it was incorporated into the actual wedding service. To allow the* BRIDE *and* GROOM *to go together to the altar, this should be done at the bottom of the chancel steps.*) Marriage is fraught with tremendous possibility of failure and success as well as pain and joy. The possibility of sorrow and of happiness is greater in married life than in single life. The person who has not made the wager of devotion cannot be hurt by the unfaithfulness of another as can the person who makes the leap of faith, nor can he know the sublimity of the joyous, majestic heights as the one who shares in depth with a trusted, compatible companion.

Are you ready in the presence of this community to declare your intention to make this venture of faith and love?

_____ are you willing to receive _____ as your wife, having full confidence that your abiding faith in each other as human beings will last a lifetime? *Answer:* I am.

_____ are you willing to receive _____ as your husband, having full confidence that your abiding faith in each other as human beings will last a lifetime? *Answer:* I am.

PASTOR'S PRAYER

Heavenly Father, who ordained marriage for your children, and endowed us with creative ability in love, we present to Thee these who have disclosed their wish to be married. May their union be endowed with true devotion, spiritual commitment, and personal integrity. O God, give to this woman, _____, and to this man, _____, the ability to keep the covenant between them made. When selfishness shows itself, grant generosity; when mistrust is a temptation, give moral strength; where misundertanding intrudes, give patience and gentleness. When suffering becomes their lot, give them a strong faith and abiding hope.

If You should bless their home with children, give them the qualities of true and wise parenthood. Make their home a shelter from that which corrupts and destroys, and may it be a school wherein they may be fitted for Thy Kingdom. Amen.

SOLOIST

"Love Never Faileth"—Root *or* "Love Is Kind and Suffers Long"—Capetown (*Couple moves to prie-dieu.*)

The Exchange of Wedding Vows

Marriage requires much of generosity, unselfishness, flexibility, Christian forbearance, and grace from both husband and wife. Under it lies the sober responsibility of home and community, but when it is supported by all the strength and commitments of love and charity, those burdens are delightful. Marriage is the mother of the world, and the nursery of heaven, filling cities and churches with the Kingdom of Christ. The reality and happiness of your marriage depends upon the inner experience of your heart and the integrity of your commitment.

As a seal of your covenant, you [each] have chosen ring(s) of precious metal, symbolizing the unity, wholeness and endlessness of your life together. (MINISTER *takes rings; to* GROOM) Will you place this ring upon the wedding finger of your bride, and say your promise to her?

GROOM

(*Giving memorized vows*) In the presence of the Lord and before these friends, I, _____, take you, _____, to be my wife, promising with Christ's Spirit, to be your loving and faithful husband, in prosperity and in need, in joy and in sorrow, in sickness and in health, to honor and cherish you, and respect your privileges as an individual as long as we both shall live. As this ring has no end, neither shall my love for you.

(To BRIDE, if a double ring ceremony) Will you place this ring upon the wedding finger of your groom and say your promise to him? [Or, if single ring ceremony, "As you receive this ring, say your promise to him."]

BRIDE

(*Giving memorized vows*) In the presence of the Lord and before these friends, I, _____, take you, _____, to be my husband, promising with Christ's Spirit, to be your loving and faithful wife, in prosperity and in need, in joy and in sorrow, in sickness and in health, to honor and cherish you, and give encouragement as long as we both shall live. As this ring has no end, neither shall my love for you. Wherever you go, I will follow; where you live, I will live; your people shall be my people, and your God my God for as long as we both shall live.

The Charge to the Couple

(*Couple kneeling*) If marriage is to be maintained at a high level of mutual benefit, the sacred aspect must be continued throughout its entire course. Two people are not married in the ceremony of an hour; you only begin to be married. What is begun must continue with growing meaning as long as life shall last.

The dangers which married life faces are so great that only a strong moral commitment and spiritual motivations can last. Mere physical attractiveness will not suffice. Only the love of God will suffice.

The Lord's Prayer

(*In unison*) Our Father, who art in heaven, Hallowed be Thy name. Thy Kingdom come, Thy will be done, on earth as it is in heaven. Give us this day our daily bread. And forgive us our sins, as we forgive those who sin against us. And lead us not into temptation, but deliver us from evil. For thine is the Kingdom and the power and the glory, forever. Amen.

The Declaration of Marriage

(*Couple stands*) Since you _____ and _____ have consented together to be married, and have witnessed the same before God and this community of relatives and friends, and have committed love to and faith in each other, and have sealed the promises with rings, I announce that God has made you husband and wife.

The Communion

Greater love has no one than this—that he sacrifice himself, and lay down his life for the other, as did our Lord. So may we partake of His Spirit as we consume the elements of His Love. (*Couple eats the bread and the cup is served to them.*) Let us pray:

Benediction

Now, may the courage of the early morning's dawning, and the strength of the eternal hills, and the peace of the evening's ending, and the love of God be in your hearts now and evermore. Amen.[4]

A General Marriage Service

(*Where a wedding is to be performed at home and it is desired to be done with dignified simplicity, the following form may be employed.*)

The persons to be married standing, facing the minister. He shall first address the company, and shall say:

Dearly beloved, we are gathered together here in the presence of God and in the face of this company, to join together this man and this woman in Holy Matrimony; which is an honorable estate, instituted of God in the time of man's innocency, and adorned by our Lord Jesus Christ by his presence and the first miracle that he wrought in Cana of Galilee, and is commended by the Apostle Paul to be honorable among all men; and therefore is not by any to be entered upon lightly and unadvisedly, but reverently, soberly, discreetly and in the fear of God. Into this goodly estate these two persons present come now to be joined; and we are here to wish them joy as they go forth to the establishment of a new home.

Then shall the minister, calling him by his first name, address the man, saying:

_____, wilt thou have this woman to thy wedded wife, to live together after God's own ordinance in the holy estate of matrimony? Wilt thou love her, cherish her, honor her and protect her in sickness and in health, and forsaking all others keep thee only unto her so long as you both shall live?

The man shall answer:

I will.

Then shall the minister say to the woman:

_____, wilt thou have this man to thy wedded husband, to live together after God's own ordinance in the holy estate of matrimony? Wilt thou love him, honor him, cherish and comfort him in sickness and in health, and forsaking all others keep thee unto him so long as you both shall live?

The woman shall answer:

I will.

When it is desired that the bride be given away, the minister shall ask:

Who giveth this woman to be married to this man?

The minister, receiving the woman at her father's or friend's hands, shall cause the man with his right hand to take the woman by her right hand and say after him, as follows:

I, _____, take thee, _____, to my wedded wife, to have and to hold from this day forward, for better for worse, for richer for poorer, in sickness and in health, to love and to cherish, until death us do part, according to God's holy ordinance, and therefore I plight thee my troth.

While they still hold each other's hands, the woman shall say after the minister:

I, _____, take thee, _____, to my wedded husband, to have and to hold, from this day forward, for better for worse, for richer for poorer, in sickness and in health, to love and to cherish, until death us do part, according to God's holy ordinance, and thereto I give thee my troth.

Then may the man produce a ring and hand it to the minister, and the minister, taking the ring, shall deliver it to the man to put upon the fourth finger of the woman's left hand, and the man, during the act of placing the ring, shall say after the minister:

With this ring I thee wed, and with all my worldly goods I thee endow, in the name of the Father, and of the Son, and of the Holy Ghost. Amen.

Then shall the minister speak unto the company:

For as much as _____ and _____ have promised to be faithful and true each to the other, and have witnessed the same before God and this company by giving and receiving a ring and by joining hands, now therefore, in accordance with the laws of God and the State of _____, I pronounce them husband and wife. Those whom God hath joined together, let no man put asunder. Let us pray.

Then shall they kneel, and the minister shall offer prayer, and the prayer may conclude with the following blessing:

The Lord God almighty, bless, preserve and keep you. The Lord with his favor mercifully look upon you and fill you with all spiritual benediction and grace that you may so live together in this life that in the world to come you may have life everlasting, through Jesus Christ, our Lord. Amen.[5]

Chapter Thirteen

Contemporary Wedding Celebrations

Over the years wedding styles and even ceremonies have changed. For a while couples liked to personalize their weddings by writing their own vows, presuming to know what obligations should be in a sacred convenant. Many found that their ideas about love, God, and the marriage relationship were difficult to articulate. There is a turning from this to acceptance of the more prepared vows.

It was fashionable for a time for brides and grooms to compose their own music and words to be sung at their weddings, accompanied by guitars and other instruments. Self-composed, romantic poems were often read or rendered with music. These are still popular, yet there is a trend toward more religious music.

Couples contemplating marriage are deeply involved with their own intense feelings. That's all very good. Yet guidelines for the marriage ceremony are designed to relieve the couple, to make their wedding less complicated, and to maintain the generally accepted community mores. These do not interfere with a couple's deepest kindness or the personalization of tender thoughtfulness or emotional considerations. These contemporary materials may be modified to meet diverse needs.

Obviously there is considerable diversity in wedding practices and social customs by various geographic regions, religious denominations, and ethnic groups. Several generations may be involved in the planning.

A Marriage Celebration

Explanation—Minister

We are together today, in the presence of God and of our families and friends, to celebrate the union of (*groom's full name*) and (*bride's full name*) in marriage. We believe God blesses the bonds of a marriage, even as Jesus blessed the wedding in Cana of Galilee with his first public miracle. Marriage is a serious relationship for (*groom's first name*) and (*bride's first name*) to form, in full partnership with God.

Opportunity to Stop the Service (*optional*)—Minister

If any person can show just cause why these two should not be lawfully joined, let him or her speak now.

Reminder to the Couple—Minister

I am going to ask you both to answer certain historic questions to indicate your readiness to enter the covenant of marriage. I will help you express your promises to each other, to love each other in Christ's name. As you speak these most important words to each other, we all are listening and supporting you with our love, hope, and joy. God blesses those who love in this way and obey his will with a wholesome, fulfilling life together.

Questions to the Couple—Minister

(*Groom's first name*), will you enter into marriage with this woman? Will you love, respect, and support her through good times and bad?

I will.

(*Bride's first name*), will you enter into marriage with this man? Will you love, respect, and support him through good times and bad?

I will.

Giving Away the Bride (*optional*)—Minister

Today these two persons are slackening their familiar bonds with parents to enter a new relationship with each other that will create a new family, a new home. It is appropriate that their parents bless their union. Who gives this woman into marriage as a blessing of her continuing maturity?

I do *or* **We do.**

(*Optional:* Who gives this man into marriage as a blessing of his continuing maturity?)

Joining Their Hands—Minister

The minister shall receive the couple's right hands into his as they face each other to speak their own promises to each other. If they wish, he may help them recite their promises, by acting as prompter.

The Promises—Couple

I, (*groom's first name*), accept you as my wife, to respect and to love, today and beyond, for better and for worse, in sickness and in health, for richer or poorer. And, as it is God's will, I pledge myself to you.

I, (*bride's first name*), accept you as my husband, to respect and to love, today and beyond, for better and for worse, in sickness and in health, for richer or poorer. And, as it is God's will, I pledge myself to you.

Exchange of Rings (*optional*)—Minister

The wedding ring is a visible sign of the marriage of (*groom's first name*) and (*bride's first name*). It is a circle without end, symbolizing the unending presence of God in this convenant. Let us pray.

Bless, O Lord, the giving and receiving of (*this, these*) ring(*s*) as a sign of love, peace, and hope. Be with this couple in the times ahead. Amen.

Wedding Vows—Couple

As he places the ring on her finger:

This is a sign of my love for you. With this ring, I seal our marriage, in the name of the Father, Son, and Holy Spirit. Amen.

As she places the ring on his finger:

This is a sign of my love for you. With this ring, I seal our marriage, in the name of the Father, Son, and Holy Spirit. Amen.

Announcement of Wedding—Minister

(*Groom's first name*) and (*bride's first name*) are just beginning to celebrate their marriage. May they continue to enjoy each other as long as they live. We have heard their promises, witnessed their sharing of rings, and shared their joy. With great pleasure, I tell you all that (*groom's first name*) and (*bride's first name*) are husband and wife together, in the name of the Father, Son, and Holy Spirit. Amen.

Pastoral Prayer for the Couple (*as they kneel*)—Minister

O Lord God, we rejoice in your presence in this holy celebration of marriage. Be with them, as they share the joys and struggles of a creative marriage. Give them a full measure of grace, so they may live in love and harmony, and grow in patience and enthusiasm. May they live here, and forever, as part of your Kingdom. Amen.

Benediction (*all standing*)—Minister

The Lord bless you. The Lord shine upon you. The Lord be gracious to you, and give you his peace. Amen.[1]

N.B. These words of liturgy may be surrounded by or combined with other acts of celebration and music, as appropriate.

Celebrating the Formation of the New Family

Address to the Congregation

My friends, you have been invited to this wedding service not in order for you to **observe it,** but rather because _____ and _____ have asked you to share in it with them. For above all, this is a service of worship which means we are here not to honor _____ and _____, but rather to give praise to God. For God is the source of all true love, including that which now binds _____ and _____ to each other. Specifically, therefore, we are here to celebrate and share in a glorious act that God is about to perform—the act by which He converts the love which _____ and _____ have for each other into the holy and sacred estate of marriage.

_____ and _____ and all of us who call ourselves Christians believe that God established and ordained marriage in order that men and women might find fulfillment and joy through sharing each other's lives in the spirit of genuine love. Because marriage is so sacred and because it is God who establishes it and not us, it is essential not only that _____ and

_____ make their marriage vows with absolute seriousness and with the intent of total faithfulness; but it is equally important that you and I pledge **ourselves** to honor their marriage and to do all we can in the years ahead to nurture and enrich it. For that surely is God's will for _____ and _____ and God's will for each of us.

Collect for Marriage (in unison)

Eternal Father, we know that you are always present with us and so, in this hour of worship, we ask only that each of us may be made more deeply aware of that presence. Especially this day we pray for _____ and _____. As they pledge their faithfulness to each other, may they realize that the strength to be faithful also comes from you. As they pledge their lives to each other, may they be guided by the example of the life you gave for us all—Jesus Christ, our Lord, in whose name we offer our prayer. Amen.

The Scripture Readings

Romans 12:1-3 (RSV)—I appeal to you therefore, brethren, by the mercies of God, to present your bodies as a living sacrifice, holy and acceptable to God, which is your spiritiual worship. Do not be conformed to this world but be transformed by the renewal of your mind, that you may prove what is the will of God, what is good and acceptable and perfect. For by the grace given to me I bid every one among you not to think of himself more highly than he ought to think, but to think with sober judgment, each according to the measure of faith which God has assigned him.

Romans 12:9-14 (RSV)—Let love be genuine; hate what is evil, hold fast to what is good; love one another with brotherly affection; outdo one another in showing honor. Never flag in zeal, be aglow with the Spirit, serve the Lord. Rejoice in your hope, be patient in tribulation, be constant in prayer. Contribute to the needs of the saints, practice hospitality. Bless those who persecute you; bless and do not curse them.

1 John 4:7-12 (RSV)—Beloved, let us love one another; for love is of God and he who loves is born of God and knows God. He who does not love does not know God; for God is love. In this the love of God was made manifest among us, that God sent his only Son into the world, so that we might live through him. In this is love, not that we loved God but that he loved us and sent his Son to be the expiation for our sins. Beloved, if God so loved us, we also ought to love one another. No man has ever seen God; if we love one another, God abides in us and his love is perfected in us.

Charge to the Couple

_____ and _____, it is absolutely essential that you realize the enormity of what you are about to undertake with these vows. Because you are human and therefore subject to error and temptation as all humans are, and because you have no idea what the future holds for you—what joys and what sorrows await you, your decisions to marry require tremendous faith on each of your parts. You must have faith in yourselves as individuals and in what you have to give to each other; faith in your relationship as a couple and in what you can be and do together; and most of all, faith in God and in his presence with you to face whatever the future holds. You must never forget that the marriage vows are not just vows of love—but they are vows of faithful love for each other grounded in God's love for you both.

Statement of Intention

_____, will you now affirm before God and before all of these persons whom you and _____ have invited to share in this service with you, that you will accept and love _____, and _____ alone, in sickness and health, poverty and good fortune, difference and agreement, in times of comfort and times of struggle as long as you both shall live?

(groom) I will.

_____, will you now affirm before God and before all these persons whom you and _____ have invited to share in this service with you, that you will accept and love _____, and _____ alone, in sickness and in health, poverty and good fortune, difference and agreement, in times of comfort and times of struggle as long as you both shall live?

(bride) I will.

The Formation of the New Family

Someone once said, "A parent's love cannot be paid back; it can only be passed on." _____ and _____ have come to the point in their lives where they must leave their families in which they knew so well their parent's love, and form a new family of their own, in order that they may take the love they have known and pass it on. It is important, therefore, that they and their parents understand and express this new relationship that they will have with each other from now on.

Will the parents of the bride and groom please stand and express their new intent toward _____ and _____ at this time?

(father of the groom) We acknowledge once again our love for both of you as our children. But now you are adults and soon you will be husband and wife together. We know that from now on your ultimate loyalty and responsibility is no longer to us as your parents but to each other.

(mother of the bride) Just as we shall always treasure the memories of the days of your childhood and youth, so now we look forward to sharing with you the responsibility that all married couples bear —that of establishing homes wherein loving persons are created.

(mother of the groom) Be assured that you will always have our love, our support, and our prayers.

(father of the bride) _____ and _____, we truly rejoice with you this day. As you begin your new family life we ask you to forgive us for any times and occasions when we may not have been for you the kind of parents we ought to have been, and take whatever good and loving things we have done for you or given to you and simply pass them on.

(bride) And we ask you to forgive us for any times or occasions when we have not been for you the kind of children you rightly wanted us to be, and please never forget that our love for you and gratitude for all you have done will always be more than words can say.

(groom) We ask you to take these roses in token of that gratitude and that love and know that we, too, rejoice in our new adult relationship with you.

(at this time the bride presents a rose to each mother)

The Wedding Vows

(groom) I call upon these persons here present to witness that I, _____, do take you, _____, to be my lawful wedded wife, and trusting in God's help, I promise to faithfully love you for better, for worse, for richer, for poorer, in sickness and in health, and to this end, I give you my word.

(bride) I call upon these persons here present to witness that I, _____, do take you, _____, to be my lawful wedded husband, and trusting in God's help, I promise to faithfully love you for better, for worse, for richer, for poorer, in sickness and in health, and to this end, I give you my word.

The Giving of Rings

_____ and _____ have both said that these rings symbolically express what they take to be the inseparability of a three-way relationship. To use their own words—"I am you, you are me, and we are one with God." These rings are outward and visible symbols, to all who see them and to these two who will wear them, of the commitment they have just made in your presence to love each other faithfully throughout their lives.

Let us pray: Bless, O Lord, the giving of these rings, that they who wear them may abide in your peace and continue in your favor, through Jesus Christ our Lord. Amen.

(groom) I give you this ring in God's name as a symbol of all that we shall share.

(bride) I give you this ring in God's name as a symbol of all that we shall share.

The Declaration of Marriage

_____ and _____ have declared before God and before you, the members and friends of this congregation, that they will live together in marriage; they have made sacred promises to each other; and they have symbolized those promises by joining hands and by exchanging rings. I, therefore, pronounce them to be husband and wife together, in the name of the Father, the Son, and the Holy Spirit. What God has joined together, man must not separate.

The Candle Lighting

(bride and groom) I am you, you are me, and we are one with God.

The Response of the Congregation

Will the congregation please stand and join with me in responsively seeking God's blessings upon this marriage.

Minister: May your marriage bring you all the exquisite excitements a marriage should bring, and may life grant you also patience, tolerance, and understanding.

Congregation: May you always need one another—not so much to fill your emptiness as to help you know your fullness.

Minister: May you need one another, but not out of weakness.

Congregation: May you want one another, but not out of lack.

Minister: May you entice one another, but not compel one another.

Congregation: May you embrace one another, but not encircle one another.

Minister: May you succeed in all important ways with one another, and not fail in the little graces.

Congregation: May you look for things to praise, often say, "I love you," and take no notice of small faults.

Minister: If you have quarrels that push you apart, may both of you hope to have good sense enough to take the first step back.

Congregation: May you enter into the mystery which is the awareness of one another's presence—no more physical than spiritual, warm and near when you are side by side, and warm and near when you are in separate rooms or even distant cities.

Minister: May you have happiness, and may you find it making one another happy.

Congregation: May you have love, and may you find it loving one another.

(the congregation may be seated)

The Minister's Charge to the Couple

The course you are embarking upon is one you have chosen for yourselves. And so you alone must bear the responsibility for what you are doing; it cannot be taken from you. It is you, the bride and groom, who as a married couple must bear the whole responsibility for the success of your married life, with all the happiness it will bring . . . but, even as you take full responsibility upon your own shoulders for what you are doing this day, so with equal confidence you may place it all in the hands of God. God has sealed your "I will" with his own. He has crowned your assent with his own. In other words, God creates out of your love something that did not exist before— the holy estate of matrimony.

Your love is your own private possession; marriage is more than a private affair; it is an estate, an office. As the crown makes the king, and not just his determination to rule, so marriage and not just your love for each other makes you husband and wife in the sight of God and man. As God is infinitely higher than man, so the sanctity, the privilege and the promise of marriage are higher than the sanctity, the privilege and the promise of love. It is not your love which sustains the marriage, but from now on marriage sustains your love.

Live together in forgiveness, for without it no human fellowship, least of all a marriage, can survive. Don't insist on your rights, don't blame each other, don't judge or condemn each other, don't find fault with each other, but take one another as you are, and forgive each other every day from the bottom of your hearts.

Such is the word of God for your marriage. Thank him for it, thank him for bringing you thus far. Ask him to establish your marriage, to confirm and hallow it, and preserve it to the end. Amen.

(From Dietrich Bonhoeffer, **Letters and Papers From Prison,** Macmillan, New York.)

The Closing Prayer

Eternal God, Creator and Father of us all—

We praise you for creating mankind male and female, so that each may find fulfillment in the other.

We praise you for all the ways in which your love comes into our lives and for all the joys that can come to man and woman through marriage.

Today especially we think of _____ and _____ as they begin their life together.

With them we thank you for the love and care of their parents, which has guided them to maturity and prepared them for each other.

With them we pray for their parents, that at this moment of parting they may find new happiness as they share their children's joy.

And now, Father, we pray for _____ and _____ themselves. Give them the strength to keep the vows they have made, to be loyal and faithful to each other, and to support each other throughout their life; may they bear each other's burdens and share each other's joys.

Help them to be honest and patient with each other and to welcome both friends and strangers into their home.

In all their future together, may they enjoy each other's lives and grow through each other's love.

Finally, we ask you to keep them faithful to you, and at the end of this life on earth, to receive them and us, into your eternal kingdom through Jesus Christ our Lord, who taught us when we pray to say together:

(From Caryl Micklem, editor, **Contemporary Prayers for Public Worship,** Eerdman, Grand Rapids, Michigan, adapted.)

The Lord's Prayer (in unison)
The Benediction

Depart with the peace of God resting upon you. Depart with the love of Christ dwelling within you. Depart with the presence of the Holy Spirit abiding with you. And may the Lord be generous in increasing your love and make you love one another and the whole human race as much as we love you. Amen.[2]

A Wedding Service in Modern English

Opening Words—Minister

We are gathered together here in the sight of God, and in the presence of these witnesses, to join together (*groom's full name*) and (*bride's full name*) in holy matrimony. Into this holy estate they have come now to be joined. If anyone can show serious cause why they may not be wed, let him now speak, or keep silent forever.

Giving of the Bride—Whoever Is Designated

Who gives this woman to be married to this man?

I do *or* **We do** *or* **Her mother and I do,** *etc.*

(*The one giving the bride away resumes his seat in the congregation.*)

Statement to the Couple—Minister

I remind you both, as you stand in the presence of God, that these vows you are about to make are serious. You are about to declare before your families and friends your faithful pledge to each other. Be assured that if you keep your solemn vows, and if you try to do God's will toward each other, God will bless your marriage, will grant your fulfillment in it, and will keep your home in peace.

Question to the Groom—Minister

(*Groom's first name*), are you willing to take (*bride's full name*) to be your wife, to live together in marriage? Will you love her, comfort her, honor and support her, in sickness and in health? Will you devote yourself to her as long as you both may live?

Yes, I am willing.

Question to the Bride—Minister

(*Bride's first name*), are you willing to take (*groom's full name*) to be your husband, to live together in marriage? Will you love him, comfort him, honor and support him, in sickness and in health? Will you devote yourself to him as long as you both may live?

Yes, I am willing.

(*The bride may hand her bouquet to her bridesmaid, to free her hands. Then the minister shall ask the couple to join hands and face each other to repeat [after him] their vows to each other.*)

The Groom's Vow—Groom

I, (*groom's first name*), take you (*bride's first name*), to be my wife, to love and to cherish, from this day forward, for better or for worse, for richer or for poorer, in sickness and in health, so long as we shall live. This pledge I make to you in good faith.

The Bride's Vow—Bride

I, (*bride's first name*), take you (*groom's first name*), to be my husband, to love and to cherish, from this day forward, for better or for worse, for richer or for poorer, in sickness and in health, so long as we shall live. This pledge I make to you in good faith.

Explanation of the Ring(s)—Minister

(*This ring, these rings*) (*is, are*) to be a visible sign to all people of the unending love that (*groom's first name*) and (*bride's first name*) pledge to each other in their Christian marriage.

Giving of the Ring(s)—Couple

(*Bride's first name/groom's first name*), I give this ring to you as an expression of my constant faith and abiding love.

Announcement to the Congregation—Minister

(*Groom's first name*) and (*bride's first name*) have joined in marriage before God, in your presence today. They have pledged their lives to each other, by joining hands and by giving and receiving ring(s). I announce that they are husband and wife, in the name of all that is holy. Let no one or anything come between these two people who have joined their lives.

(*Groom's first name*) and (*bride's first name*) realize what solemn vows they have just made. As they begin their married life together, they invite your spoken or silent prayers. Now we will have a time for informal, spontaneous prayer together. If you wish to share out loud your prayer for them, please feel free to do that. Or you may pray in silence for them. When everyone who wishes has offered prayer, we will end with our modern English Lord's Prayer in the wedding bulletin. Let us pray.

(Here may follow a reasonable period of spoken or silent prayer.)

The Modern English Lord's Prayer—All

Our Father, may all people come to respect and to love you. May you rule in every person and in all of life. Give us, day by day, the things of life we need. Forgive us our sins, for we forgive everyone who has done us wrong. Let nothing test us beyond our strength. Save us from our weakness. For yours is the authority, and the power, and the glory forever. Amen.

Dismissal Benediction—Minister

May God bless your life together. May he give you grace to love, honor, and cherish each other. May you live together in faithfulness, patience, wisdom, and joy, now and forever. Amen.[3]

A Contemporary Methodist Service
of Christian Marriage

GATHERING

While the people gather, instrumental or vocal music may be offered.

During the entrance of the wedding party, instrumental music or a hymn, psalm, canticle, or anthem may be offered.

Minister to people:

Friends, we are gathered as the Church to celebrate and praise God for the union of *(name)* and *(name)* in marriage. The bond and union of marriage were ordained by God, who created us male and female for each other. The Apostle Paul announced that where Christ is present, there is surely equality as well as unity. With his presence and power, Jesus graced a wedding at Cana of Galilee. *(Name)* and *(name)* have come here to join in marriage.

Minister to the persons who are to marry:

Christ calls you into union with him and with one another. I ask you now in the presence of God and this congregation to declare your intent.

Minister to the woman:

Will you have this man to be your husband, to live together in a holy marriage? Will you love him, comfort him, honor and keep him in sickness and in health, and forsaking all other, be faithful to him as long as you both shall live?

Woman:

I will.

Minister to the man:

Will you have this woman to be your wife, to live together in a holy marriage? Will you love her, comfort her, honor and keep her in sickness and in health, and forsaking all other, be faithful to her as long as you both shall live?

Man:

I will.

Minister to people:

The marriage of (*name*) and (*name*) unites two families and creates a new one. They ask for your blessing.

Parents or other representatives of the families, if present:

We rejoice in your union, and pray God's blessing upon you.

People:

In the name of Jesus Christ we love you. By his grace, we commit ourselves with you to the bonds of marriage and the Christian home.

Minister to people:

Will all of you, by God's grace, do everything in your power to uphold and care for these two persons in their marriage?

People:

We will.

MINISTRY OF THE WORD

Minister to people:
   The Lord be with you.

People:
   And also with you.

Minister:
Let us pray.
God of all peoples,
we rejoice in your life in the midst of our lives.
You are the true light illumining everyone.
You show us the way, the truth, and the life.
You love us even when we are unfaithful.
You sustain us with your Holy Spirit.
We praise you for your presence with us,
and especially in this act of solemn covenant.
Through Jesus Christ our Lord. Amen.

   One or more passages from the Scriptures may be read. The people may stand for the reading of the Gospel.

   A hymn, psalm, canticle, anthem, or other music may be said or sung before or after readings.

   A homily, sermon, charge, or other response to the Scriptures may follow.

   An extemporaneous intercessory prayer may be offered, or the following:

Let us pray:
Gracious God,
bless this man and woman
who come now to join in marriage,
that they may give their vows to each other
in the strength and spirit of your steadfast love.
Let the promise of your word
root and grow in their lives.
Grant them vision and hope
to persevere in trust and friendship all their days.
Keep ever before them the needs of the world.

By your grace
enable them to be true disciples of Jesus Christ,
in whose name we pray. Amen.

THE MARRIAGE

The woman and man face each other, joining hands. The following or another vow is said by the man:
In the name of God, I, (*name*), take you, (*name*),
to be my wife,
to have and to hold from this day forward,
for better for worse, for richer for poorer,
in sickness and in health, to love and to cherish,
until we are parted by death. This is my solemn vow.

The following or another vow is said by the woman:
In the name of God, I, (*name*), take you, (*name*),
to be my husband,
to have and to hold from this day forward,
for better for worse, for richer for poorer,
in sickness and in health, to love and to cherish,
until we are parted by death. This is my solemn vow.

The minister may bless the giving of rings or other symbols of the marriage:
Bless, O Lord, the giving of these rings (symbols),
that they who wear them may live in your peace,
and continue in your favor all the days of their life,
through Jesus Christ our Lord. Amen.

The giver(s) may say to the recipient:
(*Name*), I give you this ring as a sign of my vow,
and with all that I am, and all that I have,
I honor you
[in the name of the Father, and of the Son, and of the Holy Spirit].

The wife and husband join hands. The minister may place a hand or stole on their joined hands.

Minister to husband and wife:
You have declared your consent and vows

before God and this congregation.
May God confirm your covenant,
and fill you both with grace.

Minister to people:
Now that (*name*) and (*name*)
have given themselves to each other by solemn vows,
with the joining of hands, and the giving of rings,
I announce to you that they are husband and wife
in the name of the Father, and of the Son,
and of the Holy Spirit.
Those whom God has joined together,
let no one separate.

People:
Amen.

A doxology or other hymn may be said or sung. If desired,
the church registry and certificate and state license may now be
witnessed and signed.

THANKSGIVING

The Service continues with one of the following three options:

OPTION A: THANKSGIVING AND LORD'S PRAYER

Minister to people:
Friends, let us give thanks to the Lord.

People:
Thanks be to God.

Here may the following or other prayers be said:
Most gracious God,
we give you thanks for your tender love
in sending Jesus Christ to come among us,
to be born of a human mother,
and to make the way of the cross to be the way of life.
We thank you, also, for consecrating
the union of man and woman in his Name.
By the power of your Holy Spirit,

pour out the abundance of your blessing
upon this man and woman in his Name.
Defend them from every enemy.
Lead them into all peace.
Let their love for each other be a seal upon their hearts,
a mantle about their shoulders,
and a crown upon their foreheads.
Bless them in their work and in their companionship;
in their sleeping and in their waking;
in their joys and in their sorrows;
in their life and in their death.
Finally, in your mercy, bring them to that table
where your saints feast for ever
    in your heavenly home;
through Jesus Christ our Lord,
who with you and the Holy Spirit lives and reigns,
one God, for ever and ever. Amen.

Our Father in heaven,
    hallowed be your Name,
    your kingdom come,
    your will be done,
        on earth as in heaven.
Give us today our daily bread.
Forgive us our sins
    as we forgive those
        who sin against us.
Save us from the time of trial,
    and deliver us from evil.
For the kingdom, the power,
    and the glory are yours,
    now and for ever. Amen.

Then follow the Dismissal with Blessing and the Peace.

OPTION B: HOLY COMMUNION

Minister to people:
As forgiven and reconciled people,
let us offer ourselves and our gifts to God.

Here the husband and wife or representatives of the congregation may bring the elements to the Communion table.

On the night he offered himself up for us
he took bread, gave thanks to you, broke it,
   gave it to his disciples, and said:
"Take, eat; this is my body which is given for you.
   Do this in remembrance of me."
When supper was over,
he took the cup, gave thanks to you,
   gave it to his disciples, and said:
"Drink from this, all of you;
   this cup is the new covenant sealed by my blood,
   poured out for you and many,
   for the forgiveness of sins.
Whenever you drink it,
   do this in remembrance of me."
Therefore,
   in remembrance of all your mighty acts
   in Jesus Christ,
we ask you to accept
   this our sacrifice of praise and thanksgiving,
   which we offer in union with Christ's offering for us,
   as a living and holy surrender of ourselves.

Send the power of your Holy Spirit
   on us and on these gifts.
May the sharing of this bread and wine
   be for us a sharing in the body and blood of Christ.
Pour out the abundance of your blessing
   upon (*name*) and (*name*).
May their love for one another
   reflect the love of Christ for us.
Make them one flesh
   and all of us one body in Christ,
   cleansed by his blood,
   that we may faithfully serve him in the world.

Minister and People:
Through him, with him, and in him,
   in the unity of the Holy Spirit,
all glory and honor is yours, almighty God,
   now and for ever. Amen.

OPTION C: AGAPÉ MEAL

In certain settings, the agapé meal provides a transition to the wedding reception.

It is particularly fitting for weddings and provides an opportunity for corporate sharing when some members of a congregation might not wish to receive Communion.

The parts of an agapé meal are brief and may be largely extemporaneous. The minister may quote a few words of Scripture. One or two members of the wedding party, including the couple, may say a few words expressing their joy and feelings about the event. An extemporaneous prayer may be offered, and the elements are distributed. The newly married couple may aid in distributing to the wedding party and their families. The people may sing a hymn or two during this sharing.

DISMISSAL WITH BLESSING AND THE PEACE

Minister:
God the Eternal keep you in love with each other,
so that the peace of Christ may abide in your home.
Go forth to serve God and your neighbor
   in all that you do.
Bear witness to the love of God in this world
   so that those to whom love is a stranger
   will find in you generous friends.
The grace of the Lord Jesus Christ, the love of God,
and the communion of the Holy Spirit be with you all.

People:
   Amen.

Minister:
   The peace of the Lord be with you always.

People:
   And also with you.[4]

A Liberated Service

Explanation: Many of the customs which we still find in today's ceremonies ... come down to us from a time when women were considered the property of men. The "giving away of the bride" by her father, for example, is a throwback to the old custom when the bride was sold to the prospective groom. Some attempts have been made to redeem this part of the traditional wedding ceremony.

You'll note that in our service the parental blessing is obvious and the giving away of the bride is eliminated.

Prelude

[Whatever musical style is especially meaningful to the couple should be used during the service.]

Call to Worship

Minister: On this special day we gather for this special service to celebrate the wedding of two special people.

Congregation: *This is a day for singing and rejoicing, for balloons and butterflies.*

Minister: Alleluia, praise to God.

Congration: *Alleluia, praise to God!*

Processional

[Both bride and groom come in gaily together, along with their especially close friends and relatives. As they come in everyone sings the hymn.]

Hymn

"This Is the Day," from *Hymns for Now II,* edited by Steyer and Firnhaber.

(Add this verse between verses 3 and 4:

> This is the day when we share our love.
> Let us be glad and re-joice in it!
> This is the day when we share our love.)

Invocation

Gracious God, may your spirit inform and inspire this service of worship, and may it always guide the two who are to be joined in marriage today and all of us here who witness this event. Amen.

Call to Confession

Even at times of exquisite happiness like this we must be reminded that we know better than we do. Let us confess our sins before God.

General Prayer of Confession

God, this is a service celebrating love and so we are reminded of how often we have failed to be loving; celebrating the creation of a new family, and we remember how often we have taken our own families for granted and failed to see possibilities for fulfillment in them. Two people today are pledging themselves to be "all for" each other, and yet our lives are strewn with pledges seriously made and then lightly broken. We have not loved as we should; we have not been with and for our families as we could, and too often we have been untrue to our commitments. May our participation in the creation of this new relationship help us to reexamine and then renew all our relationships through Jesus Christ our Lord. Amen.

Words of Assurance

The God who created us can re-create us. This is the truth that sets us free.

Scripture Readings

The Old Testament: Psalm 150
The New Testament: 1 Corinthians 13

Contemporary Reading

[A passage from some contemporary writing that has been especially meaningful to the couple is read.]

Sermon Meditation

[Here the minister who is performing the ceremony could be invited to share some of his or her insights about the meaning of marriage or of a particular word or phrase in the marriage covenant. This might also be a time when the couple themselves would want to share with the group assembled some of their understandings about marriage and life in general.]

The Covenant of Marriage

[Where blanks are given for the names of the bride and groom, it is appropriate to alternate the order in which they appear.]

Opening Remarks

This is it, a moment packed with anticipation, when standing before God and this group of friends and relatives _____ and _____ pledge themselves to one another in the covenant of marriage.

We hope that those of you who are married will take this occasion to renew your own vows, and that all of you will share in this celebration by offering your own personal prayers for this couple ready to begin a new life together.

The Charge to the Bride and Groom

To the Christian, marriage is neither a casual nor a socially legislated business arrangement. It is a holy covenant between two persons who love each other. _____ and _____, your marriage is one of the most sacred and most treasured parts of your life. It is a celebration of all the mystery and wonder that deep love brings to living. It is also a recognition, however, that love and marriage are not always easy and that along with the tenderness, newness, and joy in a marriage, a marriage must overcome many forces that might destroy it. Love is dynamic and will fly away from a marriage which has become static and unbending. When love lives, as it does here today, it reflects the deepest and most tender secrets of the universe.

And I charge you, _____ and you, _____, with the responsibility to keep alive; to grow, to change, to maintain the capacity for wonder, for spontaneity, for humor; to remain flexible, warm, and sensitive. Give fully to each other, show your real feelings to one another, save time for each other, no matter what demands are made upon your day. I charge you to nurture each other to fullness and wholeness, realizing that each of you will need at times to bring strength and support and worth to the other. I charge you, as you grow to love each other more deeply, to discover out of this love a love for all of creation in which the mystery of your love has happened.

The Questions

[The bride and groom shall each be asked the following questions.]

Do you find within you a special love for _____ that convinces you that you want to spend the rest of your lives together?

Do you find within you the courage to resist the many deaths by which love can die?

Are you willing to love _____ into his/her unique fullness and to take the risk and accept the vulnerability of love again and again and again? (Each question is to be answered in the appropriate affirmative.)

The Blessing of the Families

Minister: Who give their blessing to this marriage and in the giving say an enthusiastic "Yes!" to this new relationship?
Families: *We do. Yes! Amen.*

The Wedding Vows

[With the bride and groom facing each other, each makes his/her offering to the other, feeling free to add personal comments to the vows.]

I offer my love; I offer my strength; I offer my support; I offer my loyalty; I offer my faith; I offer my hope—in all the changing circumstances of life—as long as we both shall live.

The Giving of the Rings

Minister: What symbols do you bring as evidence of the vows you have just taken?

The Couple: *These rings.*

Minister: These rings mark the beginning of a life journey together filled with wonder, surprises, laughter, tears, celebration, grief, and joy. May these rings be a sign to you of the continuing love you have pledged to one another today.

[If the congregation attending the wedding is small enough, the couple may wish to pass their wedding rings around to the worshippers. Each person is asked to make a silent prayer for the couple as he/she touches these tokens of their love with her/his fingers. In this way the whole congregation can actively participate in the blessing of the rings.]

[With the bride and groom facing each other, each places the ring on the other's finger and says these words.]

I give you this sign of my love, knowing that love is precious and fragile, yet strong. Whenever I see your ring I will remember all that I have pledged to you here this day.

The Response of the Congregation

As members of Christ's Church, we rejoice with you in the covenant you have made. We pledge to support and strengthen your life together, to speak the truth to you in love, and with you to seek to live a life of love for others.

A Prayer

O God, we pray that this couple and all who are gathered here will grow in the understanding and experience of love. As _____ and _____ become bound closer to each other, may they also ever be more surely themselves. To your tender and watchful care we here commit _____ and _____. In health and sickness, in abundance and want, in life and death, abide with them that they shall never withdraw from you. Through Jesus Christ. Amen.

The Declaration

You have now publicly shared your love for and special commitment to one another. Explore this love well with deep reverence. Explore it with joy and hope and perseverence. I now pronounce you husband and wife, according to the Spirit and in accord with human law.

Benediction

Today is a new beginning in the lives of _____ and _____. May God's peace and love go with them as they continue life's journey. Amen.

Recessional

"Morning Has Broken." (This song is to be sung by all as the wedding party leaves.)

Postlude

(Something joyful!)[5]

Chapter Fourteen

Special Wedding Circumstances

A Service for the Recognition of a Marriage
or
The Blessing of a Civil Marriage

(*Name*) and (*name*) have been married by the law of the state, and they have made a solemn contract with each other. Now, in faith, they come before the witness of the church to declare their marriage covenant and to acknowledge God's good news for their lives.

After the Scriptures (and sermon), the minister may say:

(*Name*) and (*name*), you have come here today to seek the blessing of God and of the church upon your marriage.

To the husband:

(*Name*), you have taken (*name*), to be your wife. Do you promise to love her, comfort her, honor and keep her, in sickness and in health; and forsaking all others, to be faithful to her as long as you both shall live?
I do.

To the wife:

(*Name*), you have taken (*name*) to be your husband. Do you promise to love him, comfort him, honor and keep

him, in sickness and in health; and forsaking all others, to be faithful to him as long as you both shall live?
I do.

Or

To the husband:
(*Name*), you have taken this woman to be your lawful wife. Since you wish to declare before God your desire that your married life should be according to God's will, I ask you, therefore, will you love her, honor and keep her, and be faithful to her, so long as you both shall live?
With God's help, I will.

To the wife:
(*Name*), you have taken this man to be your lawful husband. Since you wish to declare before God your desire that your married life should be according to God's will, I ask you, therefore, will you love him, honor and keep him, and be faithful to him, so long as you both shall live?
With God's help, I will.

The husband and wife extend their left hands:
the minister places his or her hand upon the ring(s):

Bless, O Lord, the wearing of these rings (this ring) to be symbols (a symbol) of the vows by which this man and this woman have bound themselves to each other, through Jesus Christ our Lord. **Amen.**

Or

Grant, Lord, that they who have exchanged rings may be ever faithful to one another, and continue in love, as long as they both shall live, through Jesus Christ our Lord. **Amen.**

The minister, holding the couple's joined
right hands may say:
Those whom God has joined together,
Let no one separate.

Or

(*Name*) and (*name*), you are husband and wife according to the witness of the Christ's universal church. Help each other. Be united. Live in peace. The God of love and peace be with you.[1]

Renewal
of Wedding Vows

Couples may choose to renew their wedding promises upon the occasion of their anniversary. The renewal, as with the Christian marriage, should be witnessed in a public service, in the community of the faithful.

Some couples may choose a public renewal of vows after an informal or legal separation. A renewal of vows is, of course, not sufficient for a divorced couple remarrying each other.

The renewal of vows may be celebrated at a Sunday service as a response to the Word, especially when the Scriptures and sermon deal with the subject of Christian marriage. Several couples may choose to renew their promises at the same service. In that instance, it may be desirable to have a printed text for the couples and congregation.

A. SUGGESTED ORDER FOR RENEWAL OF VOWS AS RESPONSE TO THE WORD IN THE SUNDAY SERVICE

1. Invitation to Renewal
2. Renewal of Vows
3. Congregational Response
4. Prayer of Thanksgiving
   (or the Great Thanksgiving at Communion)

The renewal of vows may be spoken extemporaneously by the couple(s). As in the service of marriage, the couple should be facing each other and speaking to one another.

The renewal of vows may be a public act of worship in its own right, and at a time other than the regular services of the church. The renewal rite may or may not include Communion or an agapé meal. The participating couple(s) and families should always be invited to develop the order and text of the service with the music director and minister(s). A printed bulletin enables maximum participation.

B. SUGGESTED ORDER FOR RENEWAL OF VOWS AS A SEPARATE
   SERVICE

1. Prelude or Other Music
2. Processional Hymn ("Now Thank We All Our God")
3. Greeting (minister, member of family or congregation)
4. Scripture Lesson(s) and Praise
5. Homily or Sermon on the Marriage Relationship
6. Renewal of Vows by Couple(s)
7. Congregational Response
8. Intercessions (Prayer for Renewal)
9. The Declaration of Renewal
10. The Peace
11. Prayer of Thanksgiving (or Holy Communion)
12. Dismissal with Blessing
13. Recessional Hymn

When the renewal of vows is a separate service, the occasion may be gladdened with a banquet, party, or picnic to which friends and family bring food, gifts, and other signs of Christian love.[2]

A Common-law Marriage

To celebrate a common-law or other relationship in which a man and a woman have been living together.

Prelude

During the prelude, the wedding party shall make all final preparations. Guests will be seated by ushers, so that all have good seats. When all is ready and the time has arrived, the bride's mother will be escorted to her place, as a signal for the prelude to conclude.

Solo (*optional*)

Processional

The groom, best man, and minister will enter from the side door, take their places, and watch the rest of the wedding party process, as is traditional. When all are in place and the proces-

sional is concluded, the minister will direct the congregation to be seated.

Word of Welcome—Minister

Welcome to the wedding of (*groom's full name*) and (*bride's full name*). Marriage is a serious commitment for two people to make toward one another. (*Groom's first name*) and (*bride's first name*) have discovered such joy and fulfillment in their love for one another that they are ready to celebrate, in your presence, what has happened and is happening between them.

Giving of the Bride—Her Father or Someone Else

Who gives this woman to be married to this man?
I do *or* **We do** *or* **Her mother and I do.**
(*He leaves to take his place in the congregation.*)

Word With the Couple—Minister

Addressing the couple by their first names: You both understand and deeply feel the profound meaning marriage has for you. You have already started to join your lives in a growing relationship that will continue to mature in the years ahead.

You chose this unique kind of wedding service to express in your own way how very much you love each other, and how very much you want your families and friends to share in your wedding.

Only the greatest courage, based on your deep and abiding love, lets you join your two lives to share an unknown future. It is an act of deepest faith to wed each other for life, come what may.

Questions to the Couple—Minister

(*Groom's first name*), in your mind and heart, is this woman, (*bride's first name*), your wife?
Yes.
(*Bride's first name*), in your mind and heart, is this man, (*groom's first name*), your husband?
Yes.

Blessing by the Minister

May God bless your marriage, grant you fulfillment in it, and let your love be a source of joy and peace, now and forever. Amen.

Exchange of Rings and Kisses
(The minister receives the rings, shows them to the congregation, and explains their purpose.)
(*This ring, these rings*) shall let everyone know that (*groom's first name*) and (*bride's first name*) are husband and wife. Let no one come between them. (*The groom places the ring on the third finger of the bride's left hand and then may kiss her. The bride places the ring on the third finger of the groom's left hand and then may kiss him.*)

Announcement of Marriage—Minister
Since (*groom's first name*) and (*bride's first name*) have come together to be married;
Since in their minds and hearts, they consider themselves to be husband and wife;
Since they have held hands and exchanged rings and kisses as symbols of their love;
Since they intend, with all sincerity, to share the future together, whatever it may hold,
(*groom's first name*) and (*bride's first name*), Mr. and Mrs. (*groom's full name*), I pronounce you husband and wife. May God bless your marriage.

Prayer for the Married Couple—All
O God, bless (*groom's first name*) and (*bride's first name*). We join with you in loving them and in wishing them well for all of life. As they live together, God, may they continue to find love, joy, and peace in their marriage. Amen.

The Kiss of Joy	Couple
Recessional Music	As All Recess
Ushering Family and Honored Guests	Ushers
Postlude[3]	

A Brief, Informal Marriage Service for a Second Marriage

Dearly beloved, we are met here in the presence of God to invoke the blessings of the Heavenly Father upon your marriage. Let us reverently bring to remembrance that marriage was instituted by God for the comfort and help of his children and that families might be trained in goodness and godliness of life. Both by his presence and his solemn words Christ honored and sanctioned it; and it is set forth and commended in the Scripture as honorable to all who enter it lawfully, seriously, and with true affection.

The minister then, asking the man to take the right hand of the woman in his right hand shall say,

————, do you before God and these witnesses acknowledge this woman to be your lawful wedded wife; and do you promise that from this day forward you will be her faithful husband, for better or worse, for richer for poorer, in sickness and in health, to love and to cherish, till death do you part?

The man shall answer, I do.

The minister then, asking the woman to take the right hand of the man in her right hand shall say,

————, do you before God and these witnesses acknowledge this man to be your lawful wedded husband; and do you promise that from this day forward you will be his faithful wife, for better for worse, for richer for poorer, in sickness and in health, to love and to cherish till death do you part?

The woman shall answer, I do.

If a ring be provided, the minister upon receiving it shall give it to the man, requesting him, as he places it upon the fourth finger of the woman's left hand to say,

In pledge of the vow made between us, I give thee this ring; in the name of the Father, and of the Son, and of the Holy Spirit. Amen.

Then the minister shall say,

Let us pray. O eternal God, Creator and Preserver of all mankind, Giver of all spiritual grace, the Author of everlasting life: Send thy blessing upon these thy servants, this man and this woman, whom we bless in thy Name; that they, living faithfully together, may surely perform and keep the vow and covenant betwixt them made, and may ever remain in perfect love and peace together, and live according to thy laws, through Jesus Christ our Lord. Amen.

Then the minister and people shall say,

Our Father who art in heaven, hallowed be thy Name. Thy kingdom come. Thy will be done on earth, as it is in heaven. Give us this day our daily bread. And forgive us our debts, as we forgive our debtors. And lead us not into temptation; but deliver us from evil: For thine is the kingdom, and the power, and the glory, for ever. Amen.

The bride and groom kneeling to receive the benediction, the Minister shall say,

God the Father, God the Son, God the Holy Spirit, bless, preserve, and keep you; the Lord mercifully with his favor look upon you, and fill you with all spiritual benediction and grace; that you may so live together in this life, that in the world to come you may have life ever lasting. Amen.[4]

Chapter Fifteen

Alternative Texts

Greetings

Dear families and friends, this is a day for celebration and thanksgiving. We are gathered to witness the marriage of (*name*) and (*name*). They have invited us to share in their public declaration of lifelong commitment to each other. We stand in the presence of God and ask for divine blessing on this solemn and joyful occasion.[1]

Or

We have come together in the presence of God to witness the marriage of (*name*) and (*name*) and to rejoice with them. Let us then consider the holy mystery into which they are entering.[2]

Or

Marriage is a joyous occasion. It is connected in our thoughts with the magic charm of home, and with all that is pleasant and attractive in the tenderest and most sacred relations of life. When celebrated in Cana of Galilee, it was sanctioned and cheered by the presence of the Lord himself; and is declared by an inspired apostle to be honorable in all.[3]

Opening Prayers

Eternal God, creator and preserver of all life, author of salvation, and giver of all grace: Look with favor upon the world you have made, and for which your Son gave his life, and

especially upon this man and this woman whom you make one
flesh in Holy Matrimony. **Amen.**[4]

Or

O God, you have so consecrated the covenant of marriage
that in it is represented the spiritual unity between Christ and
his Church: Send therefore your blessing upon these your servants, that they may so love, honor, and cherish each other in
faithfulness and patience, in wisdom and true godliness, that
their home may be a haven of blessing and peace; through
Jesus Christ our Lord, who lives and reigns with you and the
Holy Spirit, one God, now and for ever. **Amen.**[5]

Homilies

The bond of marriage was established by God at creation,
and our Lord Jesus Christ himself adorned this manner of life
by his presence and first miracle at a wedding in Cana of Galilee. This bond signifies to us the union between Christ and his
church, and Holy Scripture commends it to be honored among
all people.

The union of man and woman in heart, body, and mind is
intended by God for their mutual joy; for the help and comfort
given one another in prosperity and adversity; and, when it is
God's will, for the procreation of children and their nurture in
the knowledge and love of the Lord. Therefore marriage is not
to be entered into unadvisedly or lightly, but reverently, deliberately, and in accord with the purposes for which it was instituted by God.[6]

Or

In marriage, by the grace of God, a man and a woman become one flesh. God's purpose is that husband and wife should
give themselves to each other in love, grow together, and be
united in love as Christ is united with his church.

Marriage is ordained of God so that husband and wife, living faithfully together may help each other, come to know each
other, delight in the tender acts of love, comfort one another,
and become the best of friends.

In marriage, husband and wife become linked to each

other's families and begin a new household in the community. They may be blessed in the procreation, protection, and nurturing of children.

Marriage has serious obligations, and no one should enter it flippantly, but thoughtfully, reverently, and with mutual concurrence.

Declaration of Intention

(_____ Groom's name) Are you ready to enter this holy relationship of marriage, to accept the responsibilities of a husband; to be (_____'s Bride's name) loving, faithful, and helpful husband, whether in days of success or adversity? (The Groom answers: "I am.")

(_____ Bride's name) Are you ready to enter this holy relationship of marriage, to accept the responsibilities of a wife; to be (_____'s Groom's name) loving, faithful, and helpful wife whether in days of success or adversity? (The Bride answers: "I am.")

The Giving of Approval

Minister: Who gives approval that this marriage may proceed?

ALTERNATIVE 1

Parents (in unison): We give our approval. We rejoice in the new life you will share together. May God's blessing be upon you all your days.

People: Because Christ has loved us, we love you. Through His grace we pledge ourselves to be beside you as you enter into matrimony and a new Christian home.

Minister: Do you each promise to do all you can to support and care for these two persons in their marriage?

People: We will.

ALTERNATIVE 2

Minister to Parents: Will you give blessing to (*bride*) and (*groom*) in their new relationship? Will you support them with the love and freedom they need? Will you share your experience and wisdom with them as they seek it, as you learn from them as well?

Parents: We will.

Or

We now reaffirm our continuing love for our child, and we recognize that henceforth our primary responsibility is to both of them together.[7]

ALTERNATIVE 3

Parents: We thank God for your love which gives (makes) us a new family. We rejoice that your marriage blesses us with new bonds of trust and ties of affection. We pledge ourselves and our love to you.[8]

Pastoral Wedding Prayers

Loving God, we thank you for all families, and especially for those who stand with this couple as they establish a new home. By your Holy Spirit continue to transform their lives, day by day, so that they may grow in the grace and love of your Son and our Savior Jesus Christ. **Amen.**

Give them grace, when they hurt each other, to recognize and acknowledge their fault, and to seek each other's forgiveness and yours. **Amen.**[9]

Make their life together a sign of Christ's love to this sinful and broken world, that unity may overcome estrangement, forgiveness heal guilt, and joy conquer despair. **Amen.**

Bestow on them, if it is your will, the gift and heritage of children, and the grace to bring them up to know you, to love you, and to serve you. **Amen.**[10]

Our God, bless these as they come before family, friends, and church to affirm the choice that they have made of each other as a life companion. May their intention be to establish a home where Your love may be celebrated in the family. Grant them a seriousness of purpose, that they may be delivered from empty words and casual commitments. From the fulfillment of their vows, may they discern the varied facets of Your many-splendored love. May Your Word nurture them all the days of their lives that their dreams and aspirations may find fulfillment in the doing of Your will in all things. As we share with them in the celebration of this occasion may we all grow toward the perfection that is experienced in Your love. We pray through Him whose presence hallowed the wedding feast in Cana with a joy not known before. So may it be. Amen.

Our Heavenly Father, who hast willed the holy estate of marriage and who has taught us the way of love, we ask that Thou wouldst bless this union. As this home is established, may it be endowed with true devotion, spiritual commitments, and personal initiatives.

Give to this man and this woman the ability to keep the vow and covenant between them made. Where selfishness would show itself, give love; where mistrust is a temptation, give confidence; where misunderstanding intrudes, give gentleness and patience.

Give, our Father, times of joy, peace, and happiness. May this husband and wife in such moments acknowledge the source from which such privileges come. We realize, our Father, that life does not unfold without its bitter moments. Therefore we ask that Thou wouldst give to this union the patience to endure affliction. When suffering becomes their lot, give them a strong faith and an abiding hope. Should tragedy be woven into the fabric of this marriage, give them substance wherein they can comfort one another. May they not demand of Thee a reason for everything, but may doubt give way to trust. Help us to realize that Thou dost teach us in many ways.

If Thou shouldst bless this home, our Father, with children, give to this couple the qualities of true parenthood. Make this home a shelter from that which corrupts and destroys, and may it be a school wherein they may be fitted for life and service in the Kingdom of God.

Hear our prayer, we ask, petitioned through Jesus Christ, our Lord. Amen.[11]

Gracious God, we pray for _____ and _____ who have declared their intention to be united in marriage.

Teach them to master the high and holy art of unselfishness, that they may ever vie with each other in seeing which can give up the more, in thinking less of their rights and more of their duties; thus may they overcome the selfishness of youth in the passion of their self-surrender.

Make them wise to weigh the values of life, that they may never slay the great things for the sake of any littleness. Forbid that any tyranny of fashion or glamour of cheap fun should ever rob them of the wholesome peace and inward satisfaction which only loyalty to the best can give.

And, O God, keep them together; that most of all. May no one ever come between them—whether parent or child, or intimate friend. And, should reverses come, continually call to their remembrance that if they but keep together, no . . . circumstance shall overpower them. . . .

May their love outlast the fires of youth, warm old age, scorn death, and endure eternally in heaven.

In Christ's name we ask it. Amen.[12]

Vows

I take you, (*name*), to be my wife (husband), and I promise before God and all who are present here to be your loving and faithful husband (wife) as long as our lives shall last. I will serve you with tenderness and respect, and encourage you to develop God's gifts in you.[13]

Or

(*Name*), to you, I offer my life; I offer my
           body;
           I offer my strength; I offer my
           support;
           I offer my loyalty; I offer my
           faith;
           I offer my hope; I offer my love
              in all the changing circumstances
              of life, as long as we both shall
              live.[14]

Declaration of Marriage

Minister: (*Name*) and (*name*), by your promises you have declared yourselves husband and wife. On behalf of all gathered here I pray God's blessing on your marriage. Let us witness and sign your covenant together.

Here may the wedding certificate, marriage license, and church registry be properly signed, witnessed, and sealed.

Presiding Minister: (*Name*) and (*name*), by their promises before God and in the presence of this congregation, have made themselves husband and wife. Blessed be the Father and the Son and the Holy Spirit now and for ever.

Assisting Minister: (*Name*) and (*name*) have been joined by the love of Almighty God in the life of the Spirit of Christ, and no one must divide them.

All: Blessed be the Father and the Son and the Holy Spirit now and for ever.[15]

Holy Communion

In the ancient oriental culture, when two people entered into agreement one with the other, they sealed the covenant by breaking bread and drinking a cup together. To break faith with one with whom you had broken bread, was considered a most heinous breach of contract. When people were to be separated for a time, they broke bread and shared drink, meaning that they would be faithful to one another.

As you break bread and share this cup, you are sealing your union to one another and to the Lord, Jesus Christ who gives Himself to you.

Love one another as Christ loved you. From a loving heart our Lord offered himself upon the cross for us all. This unselfish love is symbolized in the Communion elements.

On that night long ago, Jesus took a loaf of bread, gave thanks, broke it, then gave it to his beloved, saying, "Take eat: this is my body which is given for you. Do this in remembrance of my love for you."

In like manner he took a cup of wine and gave it to his beloved, saying, "This cup is the new covenant of love in my
blood. Do this in remembrance of me."

(After the bride and groom partake, then the minister may
say:)

As Christ has loved you, so may you love one another.

The Cup of Life and
Love in Christ

An Insertion Into the Order for Marriage

Explanatory Note—This insertion may be used at some
point in the Order for Marriage following the exchange of
vows. Often transitional wording, such as the following, will be
necessary prior to and after this insertion.

Transition

Since you have confessed your commitment to one another
and stand at the gate of many years of living togther in a new
covenant relationship, it is appropriate that . . .

Insertion

. . . in these moments of beginning you share with one another this cup which shall symbolize your new life and love as
a family in Christ.

From ancient times the cup of wine has represented life's
fullness—its vast variety of content. And, as we recall from our
Lord in Gethsemane—each person must drink his own cup—
must live his or her own life responsibly under God. But yours
is now to be a shared life, and all your future experiences and
hopes are to be co-mingled as you stand before the Lord of
Life responsible to and for one another. Therefore, while re-
maining two persons, you drink of one cup.

According to the psalmists of Scripture, bitter wine will sometimes fill the cup—chafing at your life together as a scorching wind. (11:6) And, sometimes it will overflow with the wonder of happiness such as can be imagined in green pastures beside still waters. (23) And, whenever you give and receive life from one another, knowing the transforming power of Christ's forgiveness, it will indeed be for you the cup of salvation lifted up in the presence of all to the Lord's greater glory. (116)

May Almighty God bless this cup to your use as He richly blesses you in your new life together. In the name of the Father, and of the Son, and of the Holy Spirit.

(The officiant gives the cup to the groom, who offers it to the bride as she drinks from it); then she offers it to the groom. The empty cup is then given to the groomsman, who will care for it until following the wedding ceremony.)

Take this cup into your home and let it symbolize all that begins here today—and that shall continue so long as you strive faithfully to be worthy partners. If you will, make of this cup an active symbol: share it on anniversaries of this day's events, on days which will mark your own family festivals, and on those most precious days when you shall experience together the joy of mutual forgiveness and reconciliation. When children come into your lives, let this become also the Family Cup that the little ones may early learn what it is to be a family in Christ, that they may know the support of sadness shared and the exhiliration of celebrating life's marvelous surprises.[16]

Memory-Candle Lighting

As the flames of two candles are blended into one, so two personalities are blended into union with one faith, one hope, one love. May you _____ and _____ be one in name, one in aim, and one in happy destiny together.

Or

_____ and _____ you have now confirmed your union in the bond of marriage. May you be given the strength and patience, affection and understanding, loyalty and love toward each other so that the light of your oneness may never flicker nor burn out.

Or

May such fulfillment of mutual affection be yours that the light of your love will be evident to all who know you, and will reach out in concern and compassion to others.

Or

May your wills be so knit together in God's love and your spirits in His Spirit, that you may grow in love and peace all the days of your life.

Or

Now in your life together may each be to the other a strength in need, a counselor in perplexity, a comfort in sorrow, and a companion in joy.

Wedding Benedictions

The Lord bless, preserve and keep you. The Lord mercifully with His favor look upon you, and fill you with all spiritual benediction and grace, that you may so live together in this life that in the world to come you may have life everlasting. Amen.

And now may the courage of the early morning's dawning, and the strength of the eternal hills, and the peace of the evening's ending and the love of God be in your hearts now and forevermore. Amen.[17]

And now may He who walked in intimate companionship with the first human pair in the days of their innocence; and He who coming in sorrow made the marriage feast to rejoice by His miraculous ministry; and He who dwelling in your hearts can make your home a habitation of love and peace—the Father, Son and Holy Spirit—be with you evermore. Amen.[18]

As you have witnessed these vows of love, may all who are married confirm your devotion and commitments. May all who are unmarried deepen your understanding of marriage and your resolve to holy love.

Eternal God, without your grace no promise is sure.

Strengthen (*name*) and (*name*) with the gift of your Spirit, so they may fulfill the vows they have taken. Keep them faithful to each other and to you. Fill them with such love and joy that they may build a home where no one is a stranger. And guide them by your word to serve you all the days of their lives; through Jesus Christ our Lord to whom be honor and glory, forever and ever. **Amen.**[19]

Notes

1. George Hedley, *Christian Worship* (New York: Macmillan, 1953), 209, 210.

Chapter 2

1. Minister's Counseling Service Southern Baptist General Conference, 603 Texas, Dallas, Tex. 75235.

2. Oliver M. Butterfield, in *Premarital Counseling: A Manual of Suggestions for Ministers* (New York: Commission on Marriage and Home, Federal Council of Churches of Christ in America, 1945), 31, 32.

3. James R. Hine, *Grounds for Marriage* (Danville, Ill.: Interstate Printers & Pubs., 1962), 75–77.

Chapter 3

1. David L. Thompson, "The Family," *The Time-Life Family Legal Guide,* John Dille, ed. (New York: Time-Life Books, 1971), 64.

2. This chart includes information from: William E. Mariano, comp. "Marriage Information," *1984 World Almanac and Book of Facts* (New York: Newspaper Enterprise, 1984), 89; Thompson, "The Family," p. 64; Inge N. Dobelis, ed. *Reader's Family Legal Guide* (Pleasantville, N.Y.: Reader's Digest, 1981), 1130–1135.

3. *1984 World Almanac,* p. 88.

4. Ibid., p. 67.

5. Ibid., p. 68.

6. Ibid., p. 69.

7. Pregnancy Resource Books, *Deciding on Abortion* (New York: Planned Parenthood Federation of America, 1981).

215

8. Marjory Skowronski, *Abortion and Alternatives* (Millbrae, Calif.: Les Femmes Pubs., 1977), 1.

9. Thompson, "The Family," p. 50.

10. Ibid.

11. Ibid., p. 51.

12. *1984 World Almanac*, p. 92.

Chapter 4

1. Elton and Pauline Trueblood, *The Recovery of Family Life* (New York: Harper & Row, 1953), 40.

2. Roy Pearson, "No Longer Two," *Pulpit Digest* (June, 1958), 27–33.

Chapter 5

1. Elizabeth L. Post, *Emily Post's Wedding Etiquette and Planner,* Rev. ed. (New York: Harper & Row, 1982), 43, 44.

2. Based on policies of the Central Christian Church, Enid, Oklahoma.

3. James R. Hine, *Grounds for Marriage* (Danville, Ill.: Interstate Printers & Pubs., 1962), 75–77.

Chapter 6

1. Edith Gilbert, *The Complete Wedding Planner* (New York: Warner Books, 1983), 207.

2. Elizabeth L. Post, *Emily Post's Wedding Etiquette and Planner,* Rev. ed. (New York: Harper & Row, 1982), 23.

Chapter 7

1. Sources of general information: Winifred Gray, *You and Your Wedding* (New York: Bantam Books, 1980), 155–157; Edith Gilbert, *The Complete Wedding Planner* (New York: Warner Books, 1983); Elizabeth L. Post, *Emily Post's Wedding Etiquette and Planner,* Rev. ed. (New York: Harper & Row, 1982).

Chapter 8

1. Michael Daves, "Making the Wedding Service Christian," *Pulpit Digest* (January, 1965), 19–22.

Chapter 10

1. Amy Vanderbilt, *New Complete Book of Etiquette* (Garden City, N.Y.: Doubleday, 1963), 84.

Chapter 11
1. *A Service of Christian Marriage,* Supplemental Worship Resources 5 (Nashville, Tenn.: Abingdon, 1976), 52–54.

Chapter 12
1. R. C. Cave, *A Manual for Ministers* (Cincinnati: Standard Pub.), 63–68.
2. *The Book of Common Prayer of the Episcopal Church* (1949), 300–304.
3. Roy A. Burkhart, *Secret of a Happy Marriage* (New York: Harper & Row, 1949), 60–63.
4. James L. Christensen, *Contemporary Worship Services* (Old Tappan, N.J.: Fleming H. Revell, 1971), 71–76.
5. Benjamin L. Smith, *Manual of Forms for Ministers* (St. Louis, Mo.: Christian Board of Publ., 1919), 17–19.

Chapter 13
1. Stephen W. Burgess and James D. Righter, *Celebrations for Today* (Nashville, Tenn.: Abingdon, 1977), 87–89.
2. Mark H. Collier, "The Wedding Service: The Formation of the New Family," *Contemporary Worship Resources for Special Days,* Ralph E. Dessem, ed. (Lima, Ohio: CSS Pub. Co., 1973), 139–149.
3. Burgess and Righter, *Celebrations for Today,* pp. 89–92.
4. James F. White, ed., "A Service of Christian Marriage" (Nashville: United Methodist Publishing House, 1979), 3–15. Portions from the Book of Common Prayer 1979. "The Lord's Prayer" used by permission, from the Book of Common Prayer, 1979, copyright The Church Pension Fund.
5. Sharon Neufer Emswiler and Thomas Neufer Emswiler, *Women and Worship* (New York: Harper & Row, 1974), 94–101.

Chapter 14
1. James F. White, ed. "A Service of Christian Marriage" (Nashville: United Methodist Publishing House, 1979), 47, 48.
2. Ibid., pp. 55, 56.
3. Stephen W. Burgess and James D. Righter, *Celebration for Today* (Nashville: Abingdon, 1977), 92–94.
4. *A Book of Worship for Free Churches* (New York: Oxford Univ. Press, 1948), 157–159.

Chapter 15

1. *A Service of Christian Worship,* Supplemental Worship Resource 5 (Nashville, Tenn.: Abingdon, 1976), 37.

2. Ibid.

3. Furnished by the Rev. Rollin H. Neal, from *The Star Book for Ministers,* by Edward T. Hiscox (Valley Forge, Penn.: Judson Press, 1968), 203.

4. Taken from The Celebration and Blessing of a Marriage, *Book of Common Prayer* (Proposed), 429. Charles Mortimer, Custodian, Standard Book of Common Prayer.

5. Ibid., pp. 429, 430.

6. Ibid.

7. Ibid.

8. *A Service of Christian Worship,* Supplemental Worship Resource 5 (Nashville, Tenn.: Abingdon, 1976), 39.

9. Taken from the Celebration and Blessing of a Marriage, *Book of Common Prayer* (Proposed), 429, 430.

10. Ibid.

11. C. Neil Strait, *Pulpit Digest* (June, 1964), 46.

12. Adapted from "A Wedding at Countryside Christian Church," Mission, Kansas.

13. "Marriage Form," *Service Book, Part Two* (Grand Rapids, Mich.: Board of Publication of the Christian Reformed Church, 1981), II 48.

14. Sharon Neufer Emswiler and Thomas Neufer Emswiler, *Women and Worship* (New York: Harper & Row, 1974), 61.

15. *A Service of Christian Marriage,* Supplemental Worship Resources 5 (Nashville, Tenn.: Abingdon, 1976), 40.

16. Walter F. Johnson, "The Cup of Life and Love in Christ," *Contemporary Worship Resources for Special Days,* Ralph E. Dessem, ed. (Lima, Ohio: CSS Pub. Co., 1973), 150, 151.

17. Roy A. Burkhart, *Secret of a Happy Marriage,* (New York: Harper & Row, 1949), 63.

18. Horace Bushnell, from *Manual of Forms for Ministers,* Benjamin L. Smith (St. Louis, Mo.: Christian Board of Publication, 1919), 22.

19. "The Marriage Service," *The Worshipbook,* (Philadelphia, Penn.: Westminster, 1972), 67.

Bibliography

Achtemeier, Elizabeth. *The Committed Marriage.* Philadelphia: Westminster, 1976.

Bernard, Jessie. *The Future of Marriage.* New Haven, Conn.: Yale Univ. Press, 1982.

Berther, Ruth and Edward. *An Analysis of Human Sexual Response: The Masters and Johnson Study.* New York: Signet, 1966.

Blood, Robert O. and Donald M. Wolfe. *Husbands and Wives: The Dynamics of Married Living.* New York: Free Press, 1965.

Burgess, Stephen W. and James D. Righter. *Celebrations for Today.* Nashville, Tenn.: Abingdon, 1977.

Cavan, Ruth S. *Marriage and the Family in the Modern World: A Book of Readings.* 3rd ed. New York: Thomas Y. Crowell, 1969.

Christensen, James L. *Before Saying "I Do."* Old Tappan, N.J.: Fleming H. Revell, 1983.

Cleveland, McDonald. *Creating a Successful Christian Marriage.* Grand Rapids, Mich.: Baker Book House, 1972.

Clinebell, Charlotte H. and Howard J. *The Intimate Marriage.* New York: Harper & Row, 1970.

Dessem, Ralph E., comp. *Contemporary Worship Resources for Special Days.* Iowa Falls, Iowa: CSS Pub., 1973.

Duvall, Evelyn Millis. "In-Laws: Pro and Con." *People as Partners,* Jacqueline P. Wiseman, ed. New York: Harper & Row, 1971.

Emswiler, Sharon Neufer and Thomas Neufer Emswiler. *Women and Worship.* New York: Harper & Row, 1974.

219

Gilbert, Edith. *The Complete Wedding Planner*. New York: Warner Books, 1984.

Gray, Winifred. *You and Your Wedding*. New York: Bantam Books, 1980.

Hunt, Richard K., and Edward J. Rydman. *Creative Marriage*. Boston: Holbrook, 1976.

Jones, William M. and Ruth A. *Two Careers: One Marriage*. New York: AMACON, 1980.

Kammeyer, Kenneth C. *Confronting the Issues: Sex Roles, Marriage and Family*. Boston: Allyn & Bacon, 1975.

Krantzler, Mel. *Creative Marriage*. New York: McGraw-Hill, 1981.

LaHaye, Tim and Beverly. *The Act of Marriage*. Grand Rapids, Mich.: Zondervan, 1976.

Mace, David R. *Getting Ready for Marriage*. Nashville, Tenn.: Abingdon 1972.

Mace, David R. *Whom God Hath Joined*. Rev. ed. Philadelphia: Westminster, 1984.

Mace, David and Vera. *We Can Have Better Marriages if We Really Want Them*. Nashville, Tenn.: Abingdon, 1974.

McGinnis, Tom. *Your First Year of Marriage*. North Hollywood, Calif.: Wilshire, 1967.

McHugh, Gelolo. *Marriage Counselor's Manual and Teacher's Handbook for Use With Sex Knowledge Inventory*. Durham, N. C.: Family Life Publications, 1968.

1984 World Almanac and Book of Facts. New York: Newspaper Enterprise Assoc., 1984.

O'Brien, Patricia. *Staying Together: Marriages That Work*. New York: Random House, 1977.

Piccione, Nancy. *Your Wedding, A Complete Guide to Planning and Enjoying It*. Englewood Cliffs, N.J.: Prentice-Hall, 1982.

Post, Elizabeth L. *Emily Post's Wedding Etiquette and Planner*. Rev. ed. New York: Harper & Row, 1982.

Rosner, Stanley and Laura Hobe. *The Marriage Gap*. New York: McGraw-Hill, 1974.

Stewart, Charles W. *The Minister as Marriage Counselor*. Rev. ed. Nashville, Tenn.: Abingdon. 1979.

Stone, Hannah and Abraham Stone. *A Marriage Manual*. New York: Simon & Schuster, 1970.

Thompson, David A. *A Premarital Guide for Couples and Their Counselors.* Minneapolis: Bethany House, 1979.

Westoff, Leslie Aldridge. *The Second Time Around.* New York: Viking Press, 1975.

White, James F., ed. *We Gather Together: Services of Public Worship.* Nashville, Tenn.: United Methodist Communications, 1980.

Wood, Leland Foster. *Harmony in Marriage.* Old Tappan, N.J.: Fleming H. Revell, 1979.

Wright, Norman H. *Communication: Key to Your Marriage.* Glendale, Calif.: Regal, 1974.

Wright, Norman. *Marital Counseling.* San Francisco, Calif.: Harper & Row, 1983.